Jewels in His Crown

Jewels in His Crown

by
Margaret Wiinamaki

Christian Publishing Services, Inc.
Tulsa, Oklahoma

Jewels in His Crown
ISBN 0-88144-136-8
Copyright © 1989 by Margaret Wiinamaki
P. O. Box 33
Elmwood, Wisconsin 54740

Published by Christian Publishing Services, Inc.
P. O. Box 55388
Tulsa, Oklahoma 74155-1388

Dedication

Dedicated to the many wonderful women who have brought richness and beauty to my life and inspired me to write this book for others, who, like themselves, are Jewels in His Crown.

Contents

Introduction

And they shall be Mine, says the Lord of hosts, in that day when I publicly recognize and openly declare them to be My jewels — My special possession, My peculiar treasure....

Malachi 3:17 AMP

...for they shall be as the [precious] jewels of a crown, lifted high over and shining glitteringly upon His land.

Zechariah 9:16 AMP

This book declares the love of God to those He calls His jewels. Although both men and women can learn through its pages, it will probably speak most clearly to women. The words are meant to encourage both those women who at present do not feel like one of God's jewels, and those who do but long to receive His polishing touches.

The basic theme for each chapter is how women of the Bible directed their lives in a relationship with the Living God. The sub-theme in some of these life stories extends to the way these women in turn developed godly relationships with their husbands. At the end of each chapter is a summary of the truths the women of the Bible learned, applied to our modern-day lives.

1
Look to the Rock

Sarah (Gen. 11:27-12:20; 16:1-18:15; 20:1-21:13; 23:1; 24:67; Is. 51:2; Heb. 11:11; 1 Pet. 3:6.)

As Christian women there resides within our hearts the desire to love Christ and to love our husbands — and yet we must acknowledge that there are times when we do not know how to love. It is only by looking to Christ that we are able to fulfill our roles as handmaidens to God and as wives to our husbands in love.

Speaking through the prophet Isaiah, the Lord provides us a model to follow:

> **Hearken to Me, you who follow after rightness and justice, you who seek and inquire of [and require] the Lord [claiming Him by necessity and by right]; look to the rock from which you were hewn, and to the hole in the quarry from which you were dug.**
>
> **Look to Abraham your father and to Sarah who bore you; for I called him when he was but one, and blessed him and made him many.**
>
> **Isaiah 51:1,2 AMP**

In this directive God is saying: "Look to Me; look to the Rock, which is Christ, Who was with God in the beginning; look to Abraham who sired you and to Sarah who bore you."

I believe that women can take these directions literally and look first to Christ, and to Abraham, and also to Sarah as a model for womanhood.

11

Sarah

Sarai Looks to the Rock in Times of Separation

God called Abram out of the house and land of his father into a new land that He was to show him. Abram received great and precious promises: God would make him a father of many nations, bless him, and make him a blessing to all the families of the earth. God also promised that all who cursed Abram would themselves be cursed, and those who blessed him would be blessed.

Abram had a wife named Sarai who was barren — without child. He was 75 years old and his wife but a few years younger when they left Haran for the promised land. Believing God and moving in faith, Abram journeyed from his homeland to the promised land of Canaan, taking with him Sarai, his nephew Lot, and all their belongings. (Gen. 11:27-12:4.)

As Abram came into sight of the land, God pointed it out to him and again reassured him that He would give it to his seed forever. After building an altar there to God, Abram moved his caravan to the south.

Sarai Looks to the Rock in Times of Adversity

It was during this period of time that the country of Canaan experienced a terrible famine. Consequently Abram made the decision to leave for the adjoining land of Egypt for a time. It is at this point that we see the first interaction between this husband and wife:

> **And it came to pass, when he was come near to enter into Egypt, that he said unto Sarai his**

wife, Behold now, I know that thou art a fair woman to look upon:

Therefore it shall come to pass, when the Egyptians shall see thee, that they shall say, This is his wife: and they will kill me, but they will save thee alive.

Say, I pray thee, thou art my sister: that it may be well with me for thy sake; and my soul shall live because of thee.

Genesis 12:11-13

Sarai was attractive enough to cause Abram concern for his life, as the ungodly men of the land would look at her and desire her. It appears that Sarai agreed to this half-truth (she was both his half-sister and his wife) because of her love for her husband and her sense of obedience to him. We do not know why they did not believe that God would preserve them in this foreign country without their having to cover up their true relationship. They knew that God's promise included an inheritance of children and land which could not come to pass unless they were united.

Abram was certainly right about man's reaction to his wife's beauty, for the princes of Pharaoh saw her and recommended her to their master. She was brought into the house of Pharaoh and Abram was given gifts because of his "sister." However, life did not go well for Pharaoh because the Lord was displeased about this living arrangement and brought great plagues upon Pharaoh's house because of Sarai. (Read Gen. 12:10-20.)

What was Sarai thinking as she resided in the house of Pharaoh? Was it her prayers that brought the Lord's wrath upon the house? Was she angry at

Abram for putting her in this position, or was she accepting of it because she felt that by her sacrifice her husband's life was being spared? Was she calm and peaceful, or was she anxious and troubled? Later in the scriptures, both old and new, we find that Sarai is commended because, no matter what the circumstance, her faith was in God. (Heb. 11:11.)

Sarai learned to walk in faith the same way we do — step by step. She had already consented to leave her family and journey to far-off Canaan. As she dwelt in tents with her husband in a strange land, faith was something that had to grow within her. In order to arrive at the kind of womanly maturity the Lord commends, Sarai had to learn to look to the Lord, her Rock, in the same way we do today. She did not embark upon this journey with a fully-developed faith, but over the years, through many trials and testings, she learned to look to the Rock from whence she was hewn.

Sarai Looks to the Rock in Times of Insecurity

During the next few years God spoke to Abram several times, reaffirming the promise that his heir would be seed from his very own body, and that from that seed would come a nation whose numbers would be so vast they could not be counted, any more than the stars of the heavens could be numbered. Sarai also knew the promise, and as a "good wife" will often do, she decided to try to "help out" God and Abram with the fulfillment of the promise. She felt that the Lord had restrained her from bearing a child, so she asked Abram to take her maid Hagar and have a child by her, which Sarai could take as her own. Abram did as his wife said, and Hagar became pregnant.

There arose a serious complication in Sarai's plan because Hagar, proud of her new condition, began to despise her mistress who was barren. This attitude upset Sarai, and a confrontation resulted:

> **And Sarai said unto Abram, My wrong be upon thee: I have given my maid into thy bosom: and when she saw that she had conceived, I was despised in her eyes: the Lord judge between me and thee.**
>
> **But Abram said unto Sarai, Behold, thy maid is in thy hand: do to her as it pleaseth thee. And when Sarai dealt hardly with her, she fled from her face.**
>
> **Genesis 16:5-6**

Even though Sarai had given the maid to Abram, he did not claim her as his. The seed of Abram and Sarai would suffer for this breach in faith, for Hagar's son, Ishmael, became a father of a mighty nation which has warred against the seed of their son from that day to this.

When Abram was 99 years old, God appeared to him and told him that He would make a covenant with him. God said that Abram would become a father of many nations and for that reason his name would now be called Abraham. God, of course, included Sarai, Abram's wife, in this covenant because He calls two joined together in marriage as one. God's new name for Sarai was Sarah ("princess"). He proclaimed that He would bless her and give her a son. He assured her that she would be called a mother of nations — kings of people would come from her womb.

Abraham questioned his own and Sarah's ability to bear a child in their old age, urging God to accept Hagar's son Ishmael as the heir. God would not agree. He affirmed that Sarah, the true wife, would bear Abraham's child. (Gen. 17:19,21.)

Once again the Lord appeared to Abraham to tell him that Sarah would bear a son in the same season the following year. Sarah overheard the conversation and laughed to herself because she knew that her reproductive organs no longer functioned since she and Abraham were both well past child-bearing age. The Lord, knowing even the intentions of our hearts, knew what Sarah was thinking and corrected her, asking: **Is there anything too hard for the Lord?**...(Gen. 18:14). Sarah denied that she had laughed, but the Lord corrected her again, saying: "You did laugh." (v. 15.)

As Abraham and Sarah journey onward, we see another time when Abraham called Sarah his sister in order to preserve his own life. Abimelech, king of Gerar, sent for Sarah and took her into his household. However, God would not allow this offense to occur and spoke to Abimelech, warning him that this woman was another man's wife. The king restored Sarah to her husband and gave goods to Abraham in payment for the wrong he had suffered. He also gave him a thousand pieces of silver to repay him for any disgrace Sarah may have suffered. Abraham then prayed for the king and his household that they might be healed, for God had made the wives of Abimelech infertile.

Certain changes had been taking place within Sarah since the Lord corrected her for laughing. When she ended up in another man's house for the second time, the word of faith that the Lord had spoken to her began to grow. Another man's walls could not contain her, for the Lord had chosen her to be the mother of nations. The silver that was paid on her account is symbolic of the redemptive work that Christ does in our lives. Sarah was now ready to receive the promise.

Sarah Looks to the Rock in Times of Fulfillment

The faithfulness of God to Sarah is now fully revealed:

> **And the Lord visited Sarah as he had said, and the Lord did unto Sarah as he had spoken.**
> **Genesis 21:1**

Sarah did conceive and give birth to a son whom she and Abraham named Isaac ("laughter"), for God had made Sarah's laughter turn from one of unbelief to one of belief.

One more episode in Sarah's life confirms that she walked with God in agreement with His will. It was time to celebrate Isaac's weaning. A great feast was prepared for the occasion. Sarah, as mothers are often able to do, perceived that something was wrong:

> **And Sarah saw the son of Hagar the Egyptian, which she had born unto Abraham, mocking.**

> **Wherefore she said unto Abraham, Cast out this bondwoman and her son: for the son of this bondwoman shall not be heir with my son, even with Isaac.**

> And the thing was very grevious in Abraham's sight because of his son.
>
> And God said unto Abraham, Let it not be grievous in thy sight because of thy bondwoman; in all that Sarah hath said unto thee, hearken unto her voice; for in Isaac shall thy seed be called.
>
> And also of the son of the bondwoman will I make a nation, because he is thy seed.
>
> **Genesis 21:9-13**

Abraham and Sarah received the blessings of God by faith. Sarah understood God's promise for her son Isaac. Because she was walking in agreement with God on this issue, God saw her as justified in demanding that Ishmael and the bondwoman not share in Isaac's inheritance. In fact, He advised Abraham to do all that Sarah had said to do, and furthermore not to be grieved about "the lad" (note that God does not refer to Ishamel as Abraham's son) or Hagar his bondwoman (note also that Hagar is not called Sarah's bondwoman, but Abraham's). Sarah had learned to walk in faith with God — to look to the Rock from whence she was hewn.

We Look to the Rock

As we follow the life of Sarah, we discover many illustrations which will help us walk closer to God and to our husbands. Sarah was a woman with a great capacity to love: a child of God who wanted to please. In her life we see a growth in character which God desires to see in us. She did not win the plaudits of the prophets overnight, but by learning to look to God and trust Him in time of difficulty, she became a fully developed woman of God.

The process whereby Sarah became a wife, a mother and an ancient (elder) who was commended by God was no different from the one we are presently experiencing. Sarah had to walk the same path we do. She had to look to God. Those of us who are waiting to see the desire of our heart accomplished must walk in faith: **But without faith it is impossible to please him: for he that cometh to God must believe that he is, and that he is a rewarder of them that diligently seek him** (Heb. 11:6).

At times it appeared that Sarah's faith wavered, and yet she received the fulfillment of the promise of a son in her old age because she knew that the One Who had made the promise was faithful. To us, having a baby at the age of 90 is a hard thing. The things we are waiting to see accomplished seem easy compared to that occurrence. Yet, God told Sarah that nothing was too hard for Him.

Do you believe that nothing is too hard for God? Do you believe that the event you are waiting for is not too hard for Him to bring to pass? Have you found God's promise in His Word and then decided that He is faithful to perform that promise? If so, then you, like Sarah, can receive the fulfillment of your promise.

In Times of Separation

We can feel Sarah's loneliness as she traveled away from the land of Ur of the Chaldees, away from her family and the familiar scenes of her childhood. You may have experienced what it is like to move to unfamiliar territory, to leave father and mother, brother and sister and friends, to journey into a new country. Even if Sarah was excited about the promise made to Abraham by their God, and even though she and her husband were leaving a nation which worshipped false gods, she must have felt anxiety about this new unknown land to which they had been called.

What an appropriate time it was for Sarah to seek the Lord with her whole heart, to look to Him to be her friend and companion on this long and arduous trip. And if she had not looked fully to Abraham before, she was obliged to do so now, for her husband was to guide them into the land of promise as he followed God's directions.

Sometimes it takes a separation from the familiar for us to come into the oneness God has declared should exist in a marriage. If you have been geographically or otherwise separated from what is dear and familiar to you, consider that it might be God's way of giving you the opportunity to become more closely bonded to Him and to your husband.

It was probably on the journey to the promised land that Sarah's faith was tested. There is nothing like a move, or even a long journey, to test one's faith, for it is here that the members of a family must be in agreement in order for things to move forward in an orderly, synchronized manner. Did Sarah complain about the places the family stopped to rest? Was she irritable about the many inconveniences they encountered? Did she tell Abraham they should not have left their home in the first place?

Sometimes we get the impression that women in ancient times did not have to deal with the same things we do. We think that it must have come naturally for them to submit to their husbands and not question their mates' authority. What we must remember is that Sarah experienced the repercussions of the sin of Adam and Eve even as we do. Her salvation, like ours, was in looking unto the rock (God) from whence she was hewn.

Not only did Sarah look to God, but she looked to Abraham as her leader and authority. (1 Pet. 3:6.) It is always interesting to see how God puts together a man and woman with different abilities and aptitudes in order to form a unified whole. About the time we think we do not need to rely on our marriage partner, God puts us in a spot in which we must rely on our mate. At age 70, Sarah was certainly a woman established in her ways, but she was called to leave those ways behind and follow her husband as he listened to the voice of God. It does not matter whether you are 18 or 80, God can put you in a position in which you must depend on your husband.

Over the past 12 years I have learned to rely on my husband as we have spent our summers living on a boat. There have been times when we have been caught in storms out on the lake. At such times I have had to put my total confidence in God and in my husband's navigating abilities. Some of my best days, and my worst, have been spent on that boat. Sarah would probably say the same about her nomadic years.

In Times of Adversity

It is hard for us who live in a land of relative safety to imagine the fears that Abraham and Sarah must have experienced as they passed through areas populated by fierce and godless people. They did not have an embassy in the land to inquire about their whereabouts, no ambassador to inquire about their safety; they had left behind all attachments to the country of their birth. It must have been in this context that Abraham looked at his beautiful wife and asked her to pose as his sister. Sarah's feelings on the subject are not revealed, but she did appear to go along with her husband's plan.

Although we may have trouble picturing ourselves in Sarah's position, each of us has probably had to face a difficult situation in which we have felt that our husband has not made a wise choice. There is no other time when a woman needs to rely on the Holy Spirit more than when she senses that her husband has not chosen the right way to deal with a certain issue or problem.

But before she decides to act on her conviction, she must check to see if what she is sensing is the result of her own bias or negative personal feelings about the situation. The test is: "Is the way my husband is handling this situation based on scripture? Does it line up with the Word of God?"

If the answer is no, then the second step is to determine what action she is to take. It may be that she is not to say anything to her husband, but simply to bring the situation to God in prayer and allow Him to deal with it. On other occasions, it may be crucial for the wife to speak to her husband and let him know how she feels about his decision. An example from the life of Sarah is the time she demanded that Abraham remove Hagar and Ishmael from their household.

No one but God can tell us what to do in such a situation; but one piece of advice that comes from the Apostle Peter is very important because, although it does not tell us what to do, it does tell us how to do it. It concerns the way Sarah handled the situation of being brought into another man's household (as well as many other difficult situations into which she was led by her husband):

> **It was thus that Sarah obeyed Abraham (following his guidance and acknowledging his headship over her by) calling him lord — master, leader, authority.** *And you are now her true daughters if you do right and let nothing terrify you — not giving way to hysterical fears or letting anxieties unnerve you.*
>
> **1 Peter 3:6 AMP**

If anyone had an opportunity to get hysterical over situations, it was Sarah; and yet Peter cites her as an example for us to follow. What woman would not want to be a true daughter of Sarah? Sarah knew when to speak up and when to be still; and equally important, she did not give way to hysterical fears or let anxieties unnerve her.

As wives, our job is not to try to do the work of the Holy Spirit in our husbands' lives, but to look daily, and even hourly, to God for guidance and sensitivity. We are to remain quiet and peaceful of spirit even when horrendous circumstances surround us. We are able to do this as daughters of Sarah who have counted God faithful to fulfill what He has promised in His Word.

In Times of Insecurity

Women have never had so many opportunities to become involved in so many aspects of living as they do in this modern age. They have entered into and attained success in professional careers, as well as in the areas of politics, business, church and sports. Yet, even the most successful women in these fields have begun to admit that they cannot be all things to all people. In fact, many are honest enough to say that they cannot even come close. Television, newspaper, and magazine interviews reveal areas of insecurity which many are facing. These insecurities often have to do with how women feel about the kind of care they are providing for their husbands and children.

The message of the media is that the modern woman can raise a model family, be highly successful on the job, while remaining strikingly beautiful and eternally youthful. Whether they are part of the workforce or not, Christian women are not immune to these pressures. Whatever our station in life, the media still reaches us with its messages, as does the social world in which we live. A Christian woman who follows the model of the current age has even more to cope with, for in addition to all other accomplishments, she often feels that she must be a spiritual giant as well. If she is following this model, when she slips (as we all do), she feels a sense of failure.

As life continues to become more complex (as it will in this technological age), it becomes even more important for Christian women to be rooted in the image God has given them in His Word, rather than attempting to live up to a false image demanded by the world. Women feel insecure when they try to be something that God has not called them to be.

Sarah acted out of insecurity when she gave her maid to her husband to produce a child. In doing so, she brought about a "solution" that was less desirable than what God would have worked out had He been allowed control of the situation. When Sarah started trusting God, she received the fulfillment of God's promise to her.

In Times of Fulfillment

Sarah possessed at least two things that many of us might like to live with for awhile: one was beauty, the other riches. As we come into the beauty and prosperity that God has in store for us, we too must learn how to live wisely with a good thing. Remember that Sarah had both inward and outward beauty. Had she responded in pride because of these attributes, she may have ended up being stuck in Pharaoh's harem instead of becoming the Mother of Nations.

When we use beauty, riches, or any other attribute in a self-centered way, we can get "stuck in the harem." However, if we use our attributes to fulfill those works which God has given us to do, we can see them brought to their ultimate glory. Once God has prospered us and fulfilled a promise to us, He does not want us to stop there at that place or to idolize that fulfilled promise; He wants us to move on with Him.

Many Christians will testify to the fact that our faith is often tested in the good times as well as the bad. Once a promise has been fulfilled, it is easy to become complacent. Whether we pass the test in either the time of need or in the time of fullness depends upon whether we look to Christ as our Rock: **Wherefore also it is contained in the scripture, Behold, I lay in Sion a chief corner stone, elect, precious: and he that believeth on him shall not be confounded** (1 Pet. 2:6).

2
Praise Is Becoming

Leah (Gen. 29-35; 46:15,18; 49:31; Ruth 4:11.)

Many women in the Body of Christ today long for their husbands to love them in the way the Bible instructs:

> **Husbands, love your wives, even as Christ also loved the church, and gave himself for it....**
>
> **So ought men to love their wives as their own bodies. He that loveth his wife loveth himself.**
>
> **Ephesians 5:25,28**

It remains for each man to choose to love his own wife in this way. A wife can only love her husband in the way *she* is instructed. She must trust God to honor her prayer for her love to be returned.

The Old Testament women had to contend with many marital difficulties which we today do not have to face. Multiple wives were commonplace, and this arrangement often caused rivalry and discord in the households of these people. One thing has not changed; women then, as they do now, sought the love of their husbands.

Leah was a woman who loved her husband greatly and who longed for that love to be returned. Although it appears that she tried to win the affection of her husband by bearing him sons, there is something more to be learned from this woman of faith.

Her relationship with God, her trust in Him, is evidenced in the names that she gave her children. Leah's faith can give understanding to those who would seek the Lord for their own marriage.

Leah was required under the most difficult of conditions to build her marriage into one of love. May her courage and faith speak to those of today who feel that their marital situation is hopeless.

Leah

Two sisters, Rachel and Leah, were living with their father Laban in Padanaram when into their lives came their cousin Jacob from a foreign land. Neither woman's life would ever be the same.

Jacob, son of Isaac, grandson of Abraham, had tricked his father into conferring upon him the birthright and blessing which rightfully belonged to his elder brother Esau. Jacob's mother Rebekah had willingly taken part in the deception. She now had a double motive for sending Jacob to the faraway home of her brother Laban: she feared for Jacob's life because of Esau's anger, and she wanted nothing more to do with ungodly daughters-in-law such as the woman Esau had married. Both Isaac and Rebekah desired that Jacob marry a woman of the household of her mother's brother.

Jacob made the long journey to the land of his uncle and there he met Laban's daughters. In the Bible we find one short description of Rachel and Leah which has formed a certain image in the minds of readers since the time it was first recorded: **Leah was tender eyed; but Rachel was beautiful and well favoured** (Gen. 29:17).

There are many interpretations of the Hebrew word which the *King James Version* translates as "tender eyed," ranging from visually impaired to dull of eye. After studying the life of Leah, I have come to picture her with soft eyes of love. The comparison phrase "but Rachel was" indicates to me that to the beholder of the two, Rachel was by far the more outwardly attractive. Obviously Jacob thought so, as evidenced by his pledge to her father Laban: **And Jacob loved Rachel; and said, I will serve thee seven years for Rachel thy younger daughter** (v. 18).

After seven years of labor, Jaocb asked Laban to make good the marriage promise. During the night that Laban was to give Rachel to Jacob for his wife, he slyly substituted the elder daughter Leah. After the wedding, Laban agreed to allow Jacob to marry Rachel a week later, with the stipulation that he work seven more years in exchange for her hand. After taking Rachel as his second wife, Jacob loved her more than Leah.

God Is Leah's Source

The Lord saw that Leah was hated and He honored her prayers and the marriage contract by allowing her to conceive, though her sister Rachel did not. (Gen. 29:31.)

At this point, Leah's relationship with Jehovah God becomes evident. The story of her life is revealed in the names of the children she bears. Through these names, she announces God's faithfulness to her.

And Leah became pregnant and bore a son, and named him Reuben [See, a son!]; for she said, Because the Lord has seen my humiliation and

affliction; now my husband will love me (Gen. 29:32 AMP). Leah, the unloved wife, knew something very important — that God was her source. He had seen her trouble and had given her a son. It is evident that she thought that a son would make Jacob love her. But beyond that, she gave recognition to a God of the possible. She believed that *Jehovah-Jireh* ("God Who provides") would provide a way for her to receive the love of her husband.

[Leah] became pregnant again and bore a son, and said, Because the Lord heard that I am despised, He has given me this son also; and she named him Simeon [God hears] (Gen. 29:33 AMP). Leah knew that God had seen her distress and hurt, and now she recognized that He had heard her.

And she became pregnant again and bore a son, and said, Now this time will my husband be a companion to me, for I have borne him three sons. Therefore he was named Levi [companion] (Gen. 29:34 AMP). There is a greater boldness in Leah as she gives birth to a third son. She speaks out the desires of her heart as she names him Levi. Jacob will be joined to her, she declares! He will be a husband and a companion to her.

Again she conceived and bore a son; and she said, Now will I praise the Lord! So she called his name Judah [praise]; then [for a time] she ceased bearing (Gen. 29:35 AMP). Leah knew that praise was becoming to a woman of God, and she announced to all those around her that God was the One to be praised for her fruitfulness.

Leah Continues in Faith

There are times through the next few years that the prophetic names of Leah's sons do not appear to be true. Rachel remained Jacob's beloved. During these trying times, Leah had to continue to walk by faith not by sight, as all of us must do. (2 Cor. 5:7.)

Rachel cannot be separated from Leah; they were intertwined as sisters and as wives of the same husband. Leah's childbearing had not gone unnoticed by Rachel. She envied her sister and cried out to Jacob that she would die if he did not give her a child. Jacob answered her angrily, saying that he was not in the place of God Who had been the One to deny Rachel children. (Gen. 30:2.)

The next episode in the lives of this family takes place during a time when competition rather than unity prevailed. (It is important in this day of small families to recognize the value placed in those days upon having children, especially sons.) Rachel, like Sarah in Chapter 1, decided that she would have children by giving her maid (Bilhah) to Jacob. Jacob did lie with Bilhah, and she had two sons whom Rachel named Dan ("judged") and Naphtali ("wrestled"). Rachel indicated by her choice of names that God had seen her plight and had given her a son, and that in the wrestling with her sister she felt that she had won.

But Leah was not to be daunted. She followed Rachel's action by giving her maid Zilpah to Jacob, and she too gave birth to a son: **Then Leah said, Victory and good fortune have come; and she named him, Gad [fortune]** (Gen. 30:11 AMP).

Then Zilpah gave birth to another son: **And Leah said, I am happy, for women will call me blessed [happy, fortunate, to be envied] and she named him Asher [happy]** (Gen. 30:13 AMP). Leah was living in blessings. Her method of obtaining a child is not suitable under the New Covenant, but her reliance on God for blessing is still applicable. It is still appropriate to say, "I am happy and blessed by what the Lord is doing in my life." Leah knew that other women would recognize her blessings as coming from God. As we study her life, her words are being fulfilled.

Love potions have long been reputed to increase fertility. Apparently the sisters thought so, for they bargained over the mandrakes (a plant thought to be a love potion) found in the field by Reuben, Leah's oldest son. Leah revealed something of the reality of the marital situation as she contended with Rachel: **And she said unto her, Is it a small matter that thou hast taken my husband? and wouldest thou take away my son's mandrakes also...**(Gen. 30:15). The bartering was completed, and Leah gave Rachel the mandrakes in exchange for the right to sleep with Jacob. Apparently at this point in their marriage she and Jacob had ceased sleeping together.

Leah gave birth to her fifth son: **Leah said, God has given me my hire, because I have given my maid to my husband; and she called his name Issachar [hired]** (Gen. 30:18 AMP).

Either the mandrakes had long-lasting value to Rachel, or Jacob had now been reconciled with Leah, for she conceived again and gave birth to a sixth son: **Then Leah said, God has endowed me with a good**

marriage gift [for my husband]; now will he dwell with me [and regard me as his wife in reality], because I have borne him six sons; and she named him Zebulun [dwelling] (Gen. 30:20 AMP). She had made God her dwelling place, and now she could confidently say that Jacob would dwell with her as his wife.

Sometime later Leah gave birth to a daughter, whom she named Dinah, which means "judged" or "acquitted." Thus, Leah was saying, "God is my judge and He has tried my faithfulness and acquitted me."

God did not forget Rachel, and she gave birth to her first son, Joseph ("may he add"). It was at this time that Jacob, who had been forced to work for 14 years for his father-in-law, requested that he be released to return to his homeland. Laban was reluctant to allow Jacob to leave, but finally agreed upon another seven-year plan in which Jacob would receive livestock for his herds as wages for his labor.

At the end of the seven years, Jacob knew that things were not the same between him and his father-in-law. Laban and his sons were not as favorable toward him, for he had acculumated a great number of cattle, camels, donkeys and servants. However, God had directed Jacob to leave the country and return to Canaan. Jacob approached his wives about the matter, and they both agreed that Laban had been dishonest in changing Jacob's wages 10 times. They both pledged to go with their husband.

Leah could have stayed in the security of her father's home with her six sons rather than venture forth into a strange land. Her sister had Joseph, a child of her own, who was the favorite son of Jacob. Instead, despite the family situation, Leah chose to go with the husband she loved.

Jacob departed in secret, heading for Canaan with his wives, children, servants and animals. Laban was furious when he learned that Jacob had fled with his daughters, grandchildren and much of the wealth that had once been his. He also discovered that his household idols were missing along with Jacob's family. This discovery seemed to be the final straw for Laban. He might have done them much harm, but God warned him in a dream not to touch Jacob.

When Laban finally caught up to Jacob's caravan, he confronted Jacob concerning the theft of the household idols. Jacob permitted him to search his possessions:

> **And Laban went into Jacob's tent, and into Leah's tent, and into the two maidservants' tents; but he found them not. Then went he out of Leah's tent, and entered into Rachel's tent.**
>
> **Now Rachel had taken the images, and put them in the camel's furniture, and sat upon them. And Laban searched all the tent, and found them not.**
>
> **Genesis 31:33,34**

It was not Leah who needed to bring the household idols along with her — for whatever reason, whether for protection, worship or sale. Her trust was in the God of Abraham, Isaac and Jacob.

Praise Works for Leah

As the caravan drew close to the land of Canaan, Esau, the brother Jacob had wronged, came out to meet him. Jacob, not knowing that his brother was coming in peace, divided his household to protect them: **And he put the handmaids and their children foremost, and Leah and her children after, and Rachel and Joseph hindermost** (Gen. 33:2). Many have interpreted this verse to mean that Jacob gave the greatest protection to Rachel and Joseph because of his favoritism toward them. This interpretation may be true. However, it may have been Joseph, whose life was to be threatened on so many occasions in the years to come, whom Jacob was protecting. (Gen. 49:23.)

Esau greeted Jacob in love, and unity was re-established between the brothers. Jacob's caravan slowly continued to travel toward the home of Isaac, Jacob's father whom he had left over 20 years earlier. It was here that Rachel gave birth to Jacob's twelfth and final son, Benjamin ("son of the right hand"). This event completed the births of the forefathers of the twelve tribes of Israel. At the birth, Rachel died.

Leah was now the only wife of Jacob. We do not know Jacob's heart toward Leah during those years, but we do know by the names of her children that Leah was content in that love.

At the end of his long life, Jacob's request for his burial site shows that he did honor Leah as his wife:

> **And he charged them, and said unto them, I am to be gathered unto my people: bury me with my fathers in the cave that is in the field of Ephron the Hittite....**

> **There they buried Abraham and Sarah his wife; there they buried Isaac and Rebekah his wife; and there I buried Leah.**
>
> **Genesis 49:29,31**

Leah chose to love Jacob in the way she believed God intended a wife to love her husband. God blessed her in many ways; but as a wife and mother, she was doubly blessed for her son Levi became the father of the Levitical priesthood, and Judah became the forefather of the Lord Jesus Christ. Leah's blessings did not all come during her earthly lifetime but were fully realized in eternity.

Praise Is Becoming Today

Today there are many Christian women who desire to see a complete change in their family situations. However, the Lord rarely starts with the situations in which we find ourselves; instead He starts with us. Whatever the difficulty in our lives may be, God requires that we faithfully look to Him, not just for a time but until the end. He wants to find us faithful right up to the final resolution of a particular problem, right to the end of this life on earth.

You would probably agree that Leah's situation was very difficult over a number of years. However, the steps of her faith, as evidenced by the names of her children, provide us a way of dealing with difficult and even seemingly impossible situations. Through an analysis of these steps we can learn how to please the Father and walk in victory.

God Is Our Source

"The Lord saw that Leah was hated." (Gen. 29:31.) We can be assured that the Lord sees everything. He is omniscient! We may desire to have other people see our affliction, but their recognition will not help us any more than it did Job. God is the One Who sees, and it is He Who helps the afflicted.

There are some things that no human can help us with. No one could help Leah receive Jacob's love. God recognized the problem, and He helped her. She gave birth to Reuben and Simeon, and she said, "God sees and hears my affliction. Look, He has given me sons." She took an important step. She recognized that God was her source. Even though it was love from her husband that she desired, she did not look to Jacob, but to God for help. She did not trust in the frailty of man, but looked to the everlasting love and mercy of God Almighty.

When Leah sent out the birth announcements, she let everyone know that God was her source. She was saying, in essence, "Here is Reuben, God sees me. Here is Simeon, God hears my prayers." We need to make announcements also. We need to say with Leah, "God sees me and hears me. God not only has the answer to my problem, He *is* the answer to my problem."

Only God can heal a marriage. Leah recognized this truth when she named her third son Levi. She had been given the blessing of sons, but it is God Who brings a marriage together. There is no other counselor who can take the place of *Jehovah-Rapha* ("God Who heals you").

At the birth of her third son, Leah proclaimed, "Now this time will my husband be joined to me." God designed the sexual union to make man and woman one in flesh and in spirit.

It is important to see that God is in favor of your marriage being blessed. It then becomes easier for you to walk in agreement (covenant) with Him. For how can two walk together unless they are in agreement? (Amos 3:3.) If at first, like Jacob, your spouse is not willing to walk in agreement for a "whole" marriage, you may walk in agreement with God until the time your husband is willing to join in the threefold cord of husband, wife and Lord. (Eccl. 4:9-12.)

Leah gave birth to her fourth son and called him Judah. She said, "I will praise the Lord." Her sons were "little reminders" of her faith in God. How could she be downcast with a little one running around the house whose name was Praise! Leah was now entering into the fullness of the Lord for she had her eyes on Him and His majesty.

When we choose to praise God, we exchange the old dreary suit of clothes called depression for a new and joyous one called praise. (Is. 61:3.) Leah had every right, in human terms, to be angry: angry at Rachel for monopolizing her husband, angry at Jacob for not loving her and angry with God for not instantly changing the situation. But instead of putting on the garment of anger, she chose a different covering. It was a dress that becomes the woman of God. She could have worn a suit of self-pity, but she knew that it was praise that would lift her out of depression and into peace, joy and contentment. It was her choice. It is our choice also.

We Continue in Faith

Being committed to walk in faith does not mean that there will not be hard times. Leah must have experienced many difficulties over the next few years. Rachel said that she "wrestled" with Leah and felt that she had won. And even though giving one's maid to a husband was a practice of the culture, it certainly must have caused anxieties and problems within the household for both Rachel and Leah. In addition to their internal family problems, these two sisters had to deal with a father who was continually changing their husband's wages.

Leah still held to her upward climb. She knew that she had a God Who sees and hears those in affliction, a God Who joins husband and wife — and she walked in praise.

The next three steps were blessings that occur to those who walk in faith. Again it is our choice to walk in them.

When her maid gave birth to sons four and five, Leah proclaimed herself fortunate and blessed (Gad and Asher). In giving her sons these names, she was not only stating a fact, but she was expressing thanksgiving to God. Leah had a thankful heart. She was not naming her children according to what she did not have, but rather in grateful recognition of what she did have. That is what God requires of us in the faith walk — a thankful heart that counts His many blessings.

When she was reunited with her husband in sexual union and conceived her fifth son (the seventh between her and her maid), Leah said, "The Lord has given me my reward." She named this son Issachar. She was saying the same thing that the familiar verse in Hebrews states: **But without faith it is impossible to please him: for he that cometh to God must**

believe that he is, and that he is a rewarder of them that diligently seek him (Heb. 11:6).

Leah had her sixth son and named him Zebulun. She believed that her husband would truly dwell with her for she was dwelling in the blessing of God. When we dwell in the secret place of the most High, we shall abide in His loving protection. When we set our love upon God, He will deliver us. He will set us on high when we know His name and all that it will do for us. When we call upon Him, He will answer. (Ps. 91.) No problem is too great for the people of God because they have a God Who delivers.

Leah gave birth to the only daughter in the family and proclaimed that she was judged and acquitted. God had heard her prayers and answered them. She was a woman of faith, approved by God.

Praise Works

Many of Leah's blessings must have come in her later years as she watched her children grow to adulthood, and as she lived as the only wife of Jacob. We do not know the entirety of the Lord's work in her life.

We do not yet know the entirety of His work in our own lives. Unlike Leah, we have a New Covenant based on the life, death and resurrection of God's Son. Jesus, our High Priest, is now interceding for us as He sits at the right hand of the Father. Is that not enough for us to walk in full assurance of the fulfillment of the promises He has given us? If Leah could give God praise and thanks, can we not do the same? Jesus has begun a good work in our lives, and we can be confident that He will complete it. (Phil. 1:6.)

3

Trusting God to Provide

Ruth (the book of Ruth)

The book of Ruth is a love story between a Gentile woman and a man of Judah. It is the story of a loving relationship between a young woman and her mother-in-law. It is also a type of the bridegroom Jesus and His bride, the Church. It is all of these things; yet in each story there is one central theme: God provides for those who put their trust in Him. As we study the life of Ruth, we can gain valuable insight into our trust relationship with God.

The Hebrew word for a God Who will provide is *Jehovah-Jireh*. It is the name that Abraham gave to God when He provided a ram to take the place of his son on the altar of sacrifice. (Gen. 22:14.) It was to this God that Ruth and Naomi turned for provision of shelter, safety and care as they left the country of Moab where they had been dwelling, to return to Naomi's ancestral land of Judah.

Ruth

The Journey of Faith

As we begin the book of Ruth (please read all four chapters), we find that Naomi's husband and sons have died in Moab where they had been dwelling while a famine was occurring in their own country. The sons had married women from Moab;

the name of one was Orpah, and the name of the other was Ruth. Naomi, hearing that the land of Judah had begun to produce food again, set out on a journey back to her homeland with her daughters-in-law.

While on the journey, Naomi had second thoughts about taking Orpah and Ruth with her, and she urged each of them to return to their mother's home. (Ruth 1:8.) She believed that in Judah they would be looked upon as the Moabites that indeed they were — descendants of a people who in ancient times had brought shame to themselves by not helping the Israelites in their time of trouble. (Deut. 23:3,4.) Her deepest concern was that she had no more sons to redeem the family property and to marry her daughters-in-law in order to carry on the family name, as was the custom of these people.

Orpah heeded the counsel of her mother-in-law, but Ruth steadfastly clung to Naomi. With this lovely pledge she demonstrated the trust and faith that have come to characterize her:

> ...Intreat me not to leave thee, or to return from following after thee: for whither thou goest, I will go; and where thou lodgest, I will lodge: thy people shall be my people, and thy God, my God:
>
> Where thou diest, will I die, and there will I be buried: the Lord do so to me, and more also, if ought but death part thee and me.
>
> **Ruth 1:16,17**

These words are Ruth's confession of faith in God, as well as her pledge of fidelity to Naomi. She had set her course and would not be turned back. She had put her trust and confidence in the Lord God Almighty. (See Romans 10:8-13 for a Christian confession of faith.)

How sobering it is for those of us who are mothers-in-law to realize that Naomi's household must have been the example which caused this young woman to embrace the One True God and to be willing to leave everything to go to a land which she had never seen. What devotion Naomi inspired in her young daughter-in-law.

We cannot attribute all of Ruth's dedication to Naomi's example, however, for after the death of her husband and sons, Naomi became bitter. Upon Ruth and Naomi's return to the village of Bethlehem, the women who had known her asked questioningly, "Is this Naomi?" It was almost as if they were asking, "Is this the same woman?" Of course the years in Moab had changed Naomi's appearance, but bitterness also changes one's appearance. We know her condition by the words which she spoke in reply: **And she said unto them, Call me not Naomi, call me Mara: for the Almighty hath dwelt very bitterly with me** (Ruth 1:20).

No, it was not Naomi alone who inspired Ruth's devotion, for God was wooing Ruth to Him as only He can do. Despite Naomi's confession, Ruth remembered the Naomi she had learned to love during the difficult years in Moab, and she learned to trust Naomi's God Who was bigger than the present bitterness.

Preparation Time

Ruth willingly did her part to receive God's provisions. She did not wait for them to fall into her lap: **And Ruth the Moabitess said unto Naomi, Let me now go to the field, and glean ears of corn after**

him in whose sight I shall find grace. And she said unto her, Go my daughter (Ruth 2:2).

Ruth quickly found grace and favor with Boaz, who was a kinsman of Naomi's husband and a mighty man of wealth, the owner of a field in which Ruth gleaned. What a pleasing picture this young Moabite woman made as her hands quickly gathered the grain that would be food for her and Naomi. Her reputation had also followed her and had endeared her to Boaz. When she thanked him for allowing her, a stranger, to work in his fields and receive protection and food and drink, he answered her by citing her good points:

> **And Boaz said to her, I have been made fully aware of all you have done for your mother-in-law since the death of your husband; and how you have left your father and mother, and the land of your birth and have come to a people unknown to you before.**
>
> **The Lord recompense you for what you have done, and a full reward be given you by the Lord, the God of Israel, under Whose wings you have come to take refuge!**
>
> **Ruth 2:11,12** AMP

Naomi and Ruth saw God provide for their needs throughout the harvest season, as Ruth continued to glean grain in the fields of Boaz. Their trust grew as they saw God caring for them in their everyday lives.

Naomi began to advise Ruth in a plan that required a bold step of faith and trusting obedience on Ruth's part. Naomi realized that Ruth, whose name means "beautiful and compassionate," needed a home and all that goes with it. Naomi told her to go to the threshing floor where Boaz was working that night. She instructed her in detail about how to present herself:

> **Wash and anoint yourself therefore, and put on your best clothes and go down to the threshing floor; but do not make yourself known to the man until he has finished eating and drinking.**
>
> **But when he lies down, notice the place where he lies; then go and uncover his feet and lie down; and he will tell you what to do.**
>
> **Ruth 3:3,4 AMP**

It we picture the scene in our minds, we will see Ruth quietly moving through the night to reach Boaz as he made his bed next to his field where he had been working that day. Boaz had put in a long day of threshing in the heat of the day, and he had finished eating and drinking and had fallen into a deep sleep in the cool of the Bethlehem evening. He awakened, for at his feet lay a woman who had covered herself with the hem of his robe. He asked who she was, and Ruth quickly responded with an entreaty: ...**I am Ruth thine handmaid: spread therefore thy skirt over thine handmaid: for thou art a near kinsman** (Ruth 3:9).

In order to understand Ruth's response to Boaz, we must first see that she was requesting Boaz to marry her and assume the responsibility of the next of kin to her husband by carrying on the family line through the birth of children. Asking him to spread his garment or skirt over her was a way of requesting protection through the rights of marriage. A beautiful example of this practice is found in Ezekiel 16:7-14 in which God Himself performs the same act for Israel. Verse 8 reads: **Now when I passed by thee, and looked upon thee, behold, thy time was the time of love; and I spread my skirt over thee, and covered thy nakedness: yea, I sware unto thee, and entered into a covenant with thee, saith the Lord God, and thou becamest mine.**

Schofield's footnote concerning Ruth's request of Boaz to cover her with his skirt will help us understand her action even better. He says, "This action of Ruth's should be interpreted in the light of the customs of the day. It was clearly a way of letting a near kinsman know that he had not only the right but also the request to proceed with the legal steps necessary to the exercise of his responsibility. That Ruth's conduct was above reproach is indicated in Boaz's reception, protection and tacit agreement with the general evaluation of her character."[1]

Boaz's response to Ruth's request of marriage is one of the most encouraging words that a woman could ever receive. Boaz is a type of Christ, as he offers Ruth the protection and love that Christ offers women who put their trust in Him. He says, **And now, my daughter, fear not; I will do to thee all that thou requirest: for all the city of my people doth know that thou art a virtuous woman** (Ruth 3:11). Ruth's virtuous character had not escaped the notice of God, Boaz or the people of God. She was about to receive redemption from the Lord God Almighty in Whom she had put her trust.

---

[1]C.I. Scofield, D.D., *Scofield Reference Bible* (New York: Oxford University Press, Inc., 1967) p. 319.

Redemption

Naomi's prediction that Boaz would not stop until the matter was completed was accurate, for the next day he went to the city gate to publicly show his intention to redeem the parcel of land that had belonged to the family of Ruth and Naomi. In so doing, Boaz was also attempting to discern the intentions of a nearer kinsman to Ruth's husband than he was. When the other man failed to respond, Boaz then redeemed all the property that had belonged to Naomi's husband and sons. With that redemption came the right to marry Ruth. (Ruth 3:3:18-4:10.)

It is interesting to note that it was the people in the village who were the ones to proclaim God's faithfulness to Ruth and Naomi. They blessed the Lord for what He had done for these two women, for they found hope in the God Who provides for the widow and even all those who trust in Him.

Not only did Ruth and Naomi receive the blessing of Boaz's wealth and provision, not only did Boaz receive a godly wife, but they all received the promise and blessing of a son born to Ruth and Boaz. The child Obed became the father of Jesse, father of David, ancestor of the Lord Jesus Christ. The blessings gained through the trust in God of Naomi, Ruth and Boaz continue on to us and enrich us and our children.

We Trust God to Provide

Our Journey

Ruth was embarking on a new life, as you may be. Perhaps you have just started a life with Jesus, or you may be entering a new and deeper phase of the Christian walk. Like Ruth, you may have found yourself in a "new land," which could mean that you are newly married, have a new family or job, or that you have actually moved to a new community.

Ruth must have asked, as we do, "How will I get along in my new homeland? Will I be able to become a part of this new life? What is my own special place in this land?" You may feel like Ruth because you do not have the status of others around you. Do you feel that no matter what you achieve you will never be a part of the "in" group? Are you an outcast in a family or a larger social group because of the circumstances of your birth, your appearance, your lack of some attribute or another? If so, be of good cheer; God looks at the heart. God looked at the heart of Ruth — a Moabite, a member of a people despised and rejected by the Israelites by His own command — and chose her to be the wife of Boaz and the ancestor of Jesus Christ.

Ruth was determined to follow Naomi to Judah. She knew that the God Whom Naomi served was the One True God and that this God was directing her through her mother-in-law. Today we can follow the direction of the Holy Spirit Who will lead us in the way we are to go. Oprah drew back to the old land and gods, but Ruth knew that there were better things ahead, if she continued on her journey.

Our Preparation

When Ruth got to the village of Bethlehem, she did not expect a place of honor just because she had decided to take on a new life. Rather, she willingly went out with the poor of the village to work with her hands in the field to support herself and Naomi. Pride could have kept Ruth from gleaning in the fields, for this work identified her as poor, but her concern was for her mother-in-law. It was this kind of spirit that brought Ruth to the attention of Boaz. It is also this kind of spirit that brings us to the attention of our husband or husband-to-be.

Ruth showed mercy and kindness, therefore she found favor with God and man. (Prov. 3:3,4.) She demonstrated some godly principles that will help us establish ourselves in any "new land" we enter:

1. She willingly offered her service. (Ruth 2:2.)

2. She went to work in a place where the owner was known to be a righteous man. (Ruth 2:3.)

3. She was diligent. (Ruth 2:7.)

4. She was humble and not proud. (Ruth 2:10.)

5. She put her full trust in the Lord. (Ruth 2:12.)

6. She expressed her gratitude to those who helped her. (Ruth 2:13.)

At times, we begin thinking that the reason we are not moving along in an area as quickly as we would like to is because we are inadequate. We must all do what we can in any situation, but it is important to see that our adequacy is "in Christ." He is the One Who has prepared us. Naomi gave Ruth some very wise advice about how to approach Boaz. She told her to wash, anoint herself, get dressed and go down to the threshing floor.

Naomi's first word of counsel to Ruth was "Wash." Christ has already provided cleansing, anointing and clothing for us. Therefore: **Let us draw near with a true heart in full assurance of faith, having our hearts sprinkled from an evil conscience, and our bodies washed with pure water** (Heb. 10:22). We are cleansed by the pure water of our baptism and with the Word of God. (Eph. 5:26.) We have this assurance, as well as the assurance given in 1 John 1:9, that as we confess our sin, He cleanses us from all unrightousness. It is the cleanest vessel that receives the filling.

"Anoint yourself" was the second step in Naomi's instruction to Ruth as she prepared herself to meet her prospective groom. Again, anointing, like washing, was a physical act with spiritual significance. In the Old Testament, priests used oil to consecrate people to service. As believers, our anointing is already available to us: **But — you hold a sacred appointment, you have been given an unction — you have been anointed by the Holy One, and you all know [the Truth]** (1 John 2:20 AMP).

"Put on your best clothes" was Naomi's third direction. Ruth, no doubt, did put on her best clothes in honor of Boaz. As was true with the other directions, we find that this step has already been taken for us, as we see by reading the prophet Isaiah's description of the coming Christ: **I will greatly rejoice in the Lord, my soul shall exult in my God; for He has clothed me with the garments of salvation, He has covered me with the robe of righteousness, as a bridegroom decks himself with a garland, and as a bride adorns herself with her jewels** (Is. 61:10 AMP).

Finally, Naomi told Ruth to go down to the threshing floor and wait for Boaz to tell her what to do. We too must be instructed by God through His Word and His Spirit, so we can receive the overflow of blessings and become a blessing to others.

After Ruth had made her request known to Boaz, he said that he would do *all* she required. He then spoke lovingly to her about her character. We can learn by her example:

1. She listened to directions from Naomi, a godly woman. (Ruth 3:1-4.)

2. She was obedient to the directions. (Ruth 3:5.)

3. She was not only a hearer of the word; she was a doer. (Ruth 3:6.)

4. She knew God's provision belonged to her; she did not settle for less. (Ruth 3:9.)

5. She did not go after what looked good and what others saw as good. (Ruth 3:10.)

6. She had won a reputation among the city of Bethlehem because of her strength and character. (Ruth 3:11.)

7. She rested in what she had done and did not try to do more than she was supposed to do, but trusted God to provide. (Ruth 3:18.)

Our Redemption

Ruth is a type of the Gentile sinner; Boaz of the redeeming kinsman, Jesus. She and Naomi would have had quite a different life if Boaz had not followed the

Levitical law, married Ruth, and redeemed her family's land. From this story we learn that when Christ redeemed us, He brought us into His family and gave us privileges, even as Ruth received privileges through her marriage to Boaz.

If Ruth, who was under the curse of the law, could trust God to provide redemption for her, how much more can we, who are redeemed from the curse of the law, trust Him to provide all our needs?

In his commentary, F.B. Meyer says this of Ruth: "The gleaner need never again tread the fields following the reaper's footsteps. All the broad acres were now hers, since she had become one with the owner. When we are one with Christ, we no longer work for redemption but being redeemed, we bring forth fruit unto God (Rom. 7:4)."[2]

[2]Rev. F.B. Meyer, *Through the Bible Day by Day* (Philadelphia: American Sunday-School Union, 1916) p. 44.

4
Teacher of Good Things

Hannah (1 Sam. 1:1-2:26.)

The Apostle Paul gave instructions to Titus concerning the teaching of sound doctrine. Within the short letter is a specific charge to older women in the church. Paul exhorts Titus to instruct...

> **The aged women likewise, that they be in behaviour as becometh holiness, not false accusers, not given to much wine, teachers of good things;**
>
> **That they may teach the young women to be sober, to love their husbands, to love their children,**
>
> **To be discreet, chaste, keepers at home, good, obedient to their own husbands, that the word of God be not blasphemed.**
>
> **Titus 2:3-5**

When an older woman walks in holiness, she is ready to teach good things. Paul must have thought "to be sober" was at the top of the list of the desirable characteristics of the good Christian, for he not only tells Titus that younger women are to be instructed "to be sober," but so are older men, and younger men. He must have felt that this was a tremendously important character trait, for he repeats the instruction "to be sober" four times in this short chapter.

The word *sober* is often confused with somber or sad. Sobriety is not an emotion, it is a fruit of the Spirit in our lives. The Greek word *sophron* "denotes of sound mind...hence, self-controlled, soberminded."[1] The Greek word *sophronizo* means "to cause to be of sound mind."[2] The older women were to teach the younger women to be all that the word *sober* implied.

In the *King James Version* of this verse, the word *sober* bears direct relationship to the fruit of the Spirit mentioned in Galatians 6:23, particularly to the fruit which is translated as *temperance* ("self-control, moderation").

The picture of a woman who is sober, then, is not necessarily one of a woman who is unsmiling or of a sad countenance. Rather, it is the picture of a woman who is mentally and spiritually alert. She is ready to take appropriate action only after she has carefully considered a matter.

There are four reasons for all Christians to be sober:

1. *It helps us not to bring reproach to the Gospel.*

> **That they may teach the young women to be sober....**
>
> **...that the word of God be not blasphemed.**
> **Titus 2:4,5**

2. *It helps us to pray.*

> **The end of all things is near. Therefore be clear minded and self-controlled so that you can pray.**
>
> **1 Peter 4:7 NIV**

---

[1] W.E. Vine, Merrill F. Unger and William White Jr., *Vine's Expository Dictionary of Biblical Words* (Nashville: Thomas Nelson, Inc., Publishers, 1985) p. 583.
[2] Ibid.

3. *It helps us to resist the enemy.*

Be sober, be vigilant; because your adversary the devil, as a roaring lion, walketh about, seeking whom he may devour:

Whom resist stedfast in the faith....

1 Peter 5:8,9

4. *It helps us to know that Jesus is coming again!*

Wherefore gird up the loins of your mind, be sober, and hope to the end for the grace that is to be brought unto you at the revelation of Jesus Christ.

1 Peter 1:13

As the passage from Titus implies, we need to learn this quality of character. We learn by study, and prayer, and through the working of the Holy Spirit in our daily lives. We can also learn through the lives of others.

One of the women in the Bible whom I perceive to be sober is Hannah. Again, sobriety does not mean sadness, although we see both in Hannah's life. The sobriety of her life is the thing that won over the sadness and turned it into joy. (I love happy endings, don't you?)

Notice that the four reasons to be sober are numbered in the following summary of Hannah's life. Following this section is a discussion of the application of these lessons for today's woman.

Hannah ("to be sober")

Hannah, a woman of Israel living during the time of the judges, was among that company of women who had not borne children. She was one of the two wives

55

(and the most beloved) of her husband, Elkanah. Peninnah, Elkinah's other wife, had children.

Because of this situation, and Peninnah's jealousy toward Hannah, she delighted in harassing her about her childlessness. Her favorite moment to pour on the taunting was at the time of the yearly sacrifice to the Lord at Shiloh. (Perhaps you have noticed that the enemy chides us most when we are about to take part in a time of spiritual importance.) This taunting kept going on year after year. And Hannah, as we often do, became troubled because this blessing had not come forth in her life. She wept and would not eat, for she was sad.

Elkanah did not understand Hannah's grief and asked her: **...Hannah, why weepest thou? and why eatest thou not? and why is thy heart grieved? am not I better to thee than ten sons?** (1 Sam. 1:8). Obviously, Hannah and Elkanah had a close and loving relationship, else he would not have ventured to ask such a question. If Hannah answered him, we have no record of her response; rather, she turned to the One she knew could help her.

Hannah was sad, but she was also sober; therefore, she prayed unto the Lord through her tears. (Point #1.) There is a difference between "I feel sorry for myself" tears, which are emotional, and those tears shed unto the Lord. They are of the same chemical composition, yet the latter originate from a different source.

Hannah prayed, and in her prayer she made a vow to God: **...O Lord of hosts, if thou wilt indeed look on the affliction of thine handmaid, and**

remember me, and not forget thine handmaid, but wilt give unto thine handmaid a man child, then I will give him unto the Lord all the days of his life, and there shall no rasor come upon his head (v. 11.)

As Hannah sat there in the temple pouring out her heart to the Lord, Eli the priest noticed her from his seat. He came over to discipline Hannah for what he presumed was public drunkenness. She was praying silently, only her lips were moving, as she prayed for God's ears and not man's. Her behavior led Eli to believe she had been drinking, as many women of that day were inclined to do.

Hannah assured Eli that she was not drunk, as he supposed. She let him know that she was a handmaid of the Lord. Hannah knew that one reason to be self-controlled is so as not to bring reproach to the Gospel. (Point #2.) Eli perceived that she was truthful and blessed her petition to have a child.

Hannah left the place of prayer with faith and assurance. She had exchanged her sadness for a new countenance of joy.

The Lord blessed Hannah and Elkanah with a son, Samuel, whose name means "asked of the Lord." Hannah was determined to keep her vow to give this baby boy to the Lord. She did not join the rest of the family on the yearly visit to Shiloh. She knew that her time with the child was short and that soon that she would be bringing him to the temple to live.

The child Hannah dedicated to the Lord would become the great prophet and priest, advisor to both kings, Saul and David. Samuel, in later years, spoke a prophetic word that typified Hannah's actions:

...Hath the Lord as great delight in burnt offerings and sacrifices, as in obeying the voice of the Lord? Behold, to obey is better than sacrifice, and to hearken than the fat of rams (1 Sam. 15:22). Hannah had sacrificed her son, but in so doing she had been obedient to the Lord and had paid her vow. She and her husband brought the boy to Eli the priest to be given to the Lord:

> **And Hannah prayed, and said, My heart rejoiceth in the Lord, mine horn is exalted in the Lord: my mouth is enlarged over mine enemies; because I rejoice in thy salvation.**
>
> **There is none holy as the Lord: for there is none beside thee: neither is there any rock like our God.**
>
> **Talk no more so exceeding proudly; let not arrogancy come out of your mouth: for the Lord is a God of knowledge, and by him actions are weighed.**
>
> **The bows of the mighty men are broken, and they that stumbled are girded with strength.**
>
> **They that were full have hired out themselves for bread; and they that were hungry ceased: so that the barren hath born seven; and she that hath many children is waxed feeble.**
>
> **The Lord killeth, and maketh alive: he bringeth down to the grave, and bringeth up.**
>
> **The Lord maketh poor, and maketh rich: he bringeth low, and lifteth up.**
>
> **He raiseth up the poor out of the dust, and lifteth up the beggar from the dunghill, to set them among princes, and to make them inherit the throne of glory: for the pillars of the earth are the Lord's, and he hath set the world upon them.**

> **He will keep the feet of his saints, and the wicked shall be silent in darkness; for by strength shall no man prevail.**
>
> **The adversaries of the Lord shall be broken to pieces; out of heaven shall he thunder upon them: the Lord shall judge the ends of the earth; and he shall give strength unto his king, and exalt the horn of his anointed.**
>
> **1 Samuel 2:1-10**

Hannah's inspired prayer to the Lord tells us a great deal about this woman. It is here that we see the depth of Hannah's reverence of the Lord. Many writers believe that the prophetic song of Hannah was an inspiration to Mary, the mother of Jesus, whose prayer is found in Luke 1:46-55. Mary rejoiced, for she was to give birth to a Son Who was to be given as the perfect sacrifice for the whole world.

In her spiritual song, Hannah proclaims that she no longer must be silent (nowhere do we see that she answered Peninnah back for her tauntings). God had heard her prayer, and she gives Him the praise. She understood that to be sober is to resist the real enemy, Satan. (Point #3.) Not only are Hannah's enemies broken, but more importantly, God's enemies are broken. Hannah knew that Peninnah was not the one she needed to resist; rather, it was the power of the Enemy which she had to resist. (Eph. 6:12.)

In the last verse of Hannah's prayer, she demonstrates her knowledge of the coming Messiah. (Point #4.) She said: **...the Lord shall judge the ends of the earth; and he shall give strength unto his king, and exalt the horn of his anointed** (v. 10). Hannah prophesied of the soon-coming King Saul, whom Samuel was to anoint as the first king of the

Israelite nation. But, more importantly, she prophesied of the King of kings Who was yet to come.

Teacher of Good Things Today

Helps Us Not to Bring Reproach to the Gospel

Today, we too, need to examine how we can bring honor rather than reproach to the Gospel. This learning process should not begin with a list of do nots, although certainly there are some. The best way to bring honor rather than reproach to the Gospel is to be God-conscious rather than sin-conscious. When we cherish God and the things of God, it puts us in a position of reverence rather than reproach.

In the list in Titus of good things that will keep us from bringing reproach to the Gospel, we find one to be discretion. What is your definition of discretion? Movies and television suggest that a discreet woman is one who can have an extra-martial affair in secret. This is definitely not what Paul had in mind. Webster's dictionary defines *discreet* as "careful about what one says or does; prudent; keeping silent or preserving confidence when necessary." Disretion is obviously something valuable, for we read in the Bible: **Discretion shall preserve thee, understanding shall keep thee** (Prov. 2:11.)

It is important for us today to keep confidences — to keep to ourselves those things that have been shared with us. Discretion also means keeping our conversation pure and our conduct right.

Helps Us to Pray

Being sober helps us to pray. When troubles surround us, the wisest thing to do is to go into our bedroom, kneel down and pray. Instead, we often prefer to plunge our hands into soapy water and scrub whatever is in sight, or take a long walk, or call a friend. However, it is prayer that has a long-lasting effect. It changes us, smooths over ruffled relationships, opens up avenues of God's provision and accomplishes what nothing else can. Hannah prayed with purpose, and she gave birth to a son. When we pray with purpose, we too can give birth to the desires of our hearts.

Helps Us to Resist the Enemy

Women must learn to resist the enemy in their own lives and in their families' lives. Certainly we receive protection from mothers and fathers, husbands and pastors, but no one can resist Satan in our lives as we can. The family is the place where Satan would most like to win ground. We must order him out of our territory and not let him take one inch.

There is an old saying about someone who is bold: "Give him an inch, and he will take a mile." That is certainly what the enemies of the family will do if they are allowed to. Christian women must stay sober to watch that their families do not give into the enemy. We do that first by resisting him in our own lives.

Helps Us to Know that Jesus Is Coming Again

In this world of vast material riches, we often get our eyes on those things which we desire for ourselves and our family, things that are transient in terms of eternity — college educations, homes, cars, clothing and entertainment. We can be deceived into working and praying with only these rewards in mind, getting our eyes off of the words of Jesus which remind us to look for His return.

As good parents, we don't want our children to fall behind in any good thing, whether it is a position on a team or a good job. Yet if we are not careful, we can fall behind in seeking those things which have eternal value. In this giddy, "if it feels good, do it" world, it takes sobriety to watch and pray for our Savior's return.

5
Wise Are Her Ways

The Proverbs 31 Woman

Unlike many other women in the Bible, the woman described in Proverbs 31 does not have a name. This chapter is supposed to have been written by King Lemeul, which many writers believe is a pen name for King Solomon who was writing about his mother Bathsheba.

In this last chapter of the book of Proverbs, the writer is drawing a picture of the type woman a young man should seek as his wife. Whoever the woman is, she is the culmination of womanly wisdom. Her life is a mirror reflection of the Word of God into which we may look today.

The Amplified Bible version of Proverbs 31, beginning at verse 10 and continuing through to the end of the chapter, gives us a richer, fuller meaning of the text. (To further expand your study, read this passage in several different Bible versions.)

Proverbs 31

10. A capable, intelligent and virtuous woman, who is he who can find her? She is far more precious than jewels, and her value is far above rubies or pearls.

11. The heart of her husband trusts in her confidently and relies on and believes in her safely,

so that he has no lack of honest gain or need of dishonest spoil.

12. She will comfort, encourage and do him only good as long as there is life within her.

13. She seeks out the wool and flax and works with willing hands to develop it.

14. She is like the merchant ships loaded with foodstuffs, she brings her household's food from a far [country].

15. She rises while yet it is night and gets spiritual food for her household and assigns her maids their tasks.

16. She considers a new field before she buys or accepts it — expanding prudently [and not courting neglect of her present duties by assuming others]. With her savings [of time and strength] she plants fruitful vines in her vineyard.

17. She girds herself with strength [spiritual, mental and physical fitness for her God-given task] and makes her arms strong and firm.

18. She tastes and sees that her gain from work [with and for God] is good; her lamp goes not out; but it burns on continually through the night [of trouble, privation or sorrow, warning away fear, doubt and distrust].

19. She lays her hands to the spindle, and her hands hold the distaff.

20. She opens her hand to the poor; yes, she reaches out her filled hands to the needy [whether in body, mind or spirit].

21. She fears not the snow for her family, for all her household are doubly clothed in scarlet.

22. She makes for herself coverlets, cushions and rugs of tapestry. Her clothing is of linen, pure white and fine, and of purple [such as that of which the clothing of the priests and the hallowed cloths of the temple are made].

23. Her husband is known in the city's gates, when he sits among the elders of the land.

24. She makes fine linen garments and leads others to buy them; she delivers to the merchants girdles [or sashes that free one for service].

25. Strength and dignity are her clothing and her position is strong and secure. She rejoices over the future — the latter day or time to come [knowing that she and her family are in readiness for it]!

26. She opens her mouth with skillful and godly Wisdom, and in her tongue is the law of kindness — giving counsel and instruction.

27. She looks well to how things go in her household, and the bread of idleness [gossip, discontent and self-pity] she will not eat.

28. Her children rise up and call her blessed [happy, fortunate and to be envied]; and her husband boasts of and praises her, saying,

29. Many daughters have done virtuously, nobly and well [with the strength of character that is steadfast in goodness] but you excel them all.

30. Charm and grace are deceptive, and beauty is vain [because it is not lasting], but a woman who reverently and worshipfully fears the Lord, she shall be praised!

31. Give her of the fruit of her hands, and let her own works praise her in the gates of the city!

Proverbs 31:10-31 AMP

Today's Proverbs 31 Woman

Valuable (v. 10.)

Whoever finds a wife like the one described above finds enormous wealth — in fact, a priceless treasure. This is but one scripture in the Bible that places a high value on the woman of God.

"Who is a capable, intelligent and virtuous woman?" She is a righteous woman who conducts her affairs in an effectual, thoughtful way, a way that is right before God. Because of this fact, she is not only precious and highly valuable to the prosperity of her husband, but she is precious to God, even as we are because of our right standing in Christ: **For he (God) hath made him (Jesus) to be sin for us, who knew no sin: that we might be made the righteousness of God in him** (2 Cor. 5:21).

If you are thinking that the word *virtuous* does not describe you, it is time to begin believing that you are who the verse above says you are — the righteousness of God in Christ. Furthermore, as you continue to conform your life to Christ, you will increase in virtue, for He is virtue and you will become increasingly like Him.

The woman of God is not only virtuous, but her intelligence and resulting capability show her to be a multi-faceted person. You may not feel that you possess intelligence and capability, but you can have these qualities because it is the Lord Who gives understanding. (Job 32:8.) The spirit of wisdom and understanding rests on Jesus (Is. 11:2.); therefore, these attributes are available to us as we receive His Spirit.

We can learn from the capable women in our lives, but we insult God when we compare ourselves to them in a depreciating way. Remember, synthetic jewels are still made with the same formula; genuine ones are unique in their God-created beauty. Remember also that it takes a great deal of polishing and buffing to bring luster to one's character — polishing which only time and effort can produce. If you are not shining the way you would like, do not worry; God is not finished with you yet.

Trustworthy (v. 11.)

The woman who has all of these character traits is more valuable than a ruby, one of the most precious and beautiful of jewels. A ruby is inanimate; although it may increase in value as it sets in the jewel case, it can never compare to the worth of a godly wife who continues to bring increase in spiritual and material riches to her husband and family. The husband of the virtuous woman will not be forced to look for dishonest riches, because he is blessed through his wife.

Comforting (v. 12.)

One of the most difficult things to do is to bring comfort and encouragement to another person when we ourselves are longing for these same blessings. To be able to put aside her own desires which are clamoring within and to ask, "What is it that my husband needs" is a sign of a mature woman — regardless of her age. Our decision to put the needs of our mate first allows the Holy Spirit to work within his life. When we give comfort and encouragement to others, then, like a boomerang, comfort and encouragement will come back to us (perhaps not in the same form we have given them, but God will provide)!

This verse has special meaning to me: A few months before my youngest son was to marry, I became concerned one day about the care and love his future wife would show him, even though I knew her to be a Christian woman. The phrase from Proverbs 31:11 — "she will do him good as long as she lives" — was the answer I received from the Lord as I brought my concern to Him. This was an assurance to me for my son's marriage.

Mothers need to pray for a Proverbs 31 woman for each of their sons.

Productive (v. 13.)

In this verse we can picture a woman who does not wait to be told what to do, nor expect others to do everything for her. She takes the initiative in her role as wife and mother. Even as Ruth worked diligently in the barley fields to support herself and her mother-in-law Naomi, so does this woman help to provide the materials that will bring enjoyment and warmth to her family.

The warmth of wool made it highly valued in Israel for garments for cool evenings. The return to cottons and woolens in clothing has demonstrated that we too seek warmth and comfort in the various seasons. Wool also symbolizes protection against evil forces. Wise women recognize that their families need protective covering. Praying in the name of Jesus, they cover their families with the Word of God and give thanks for the saving, redemptive blood of Jesus.

Fruitful (v. 14.)

Several images of the virtuous woman can be seen in this verse. Perhaps she lived on the Mediterranean coast of Israel, and, like the merchant ships she saw coming into the harbor from afar, she bore a cargo of good food to nourish and sustain her faimly. Or perhaps she lived in the desert region, and, like the caravans of old, she provided a variety of the good things her family enjoyed.

Shopping in today's American supermarkets is a delight! Never have we had such a plentiful supply of appealing and nutritious food from the countries of the world as is available to us today. This variety enables us to give our families tasty delights, as well as an appreciation of the culture of other nations as we enjoy their foods — tonight Mexican, tomorrow Cantonese. Thanks to modern technology, we can avail ourselves of these foods with much less effort than the Israelites of Solomon's time.

As closely tied as food and wives are, we miss the point if we see no more than an abundance of food in cupboards and refrigerator. Rarely does a divorce occur because of a lack of food preparation skills. It is spiritual food that hearts hunger for.

There is an essential foodstuff with which a wife can be loaded down, food that will never grow stale nor cease to nourish. That food is the fruit of the Spirit described in Galatians 5:22,23. As she prays and grows in the Spirit, the godly woman produces a harvest of good things, both material and spiritual, for her family.

Alert (v. 15.)

The virtuous woman rises early to seek God and to pray for the "manna" that will nourish her family that day. As spiritual people, we know that bread is not enough; we need the Word of God in our lives. (Deut. 8:3; Matt. 4:4; Luke 4:4.) We need the Living Word — Jesus. (John 6:57.)

The fruits that were described in the section above in verse 14 can grow best in the climate produced by the act of the will that is performed by the woman in verse 15.

Are you aware that "rising while yet it is night" is an act of your will? Your body will not want to rise for food of any kind; however, early morning is an important time to ask the Lord to give you your daily bread. The psalmist David said: **My voice shalt thou hear in the morning, O Lord; in the morning will I direct my prayer unto thee, and will look up** (Ps. 5:3). If you have a stirring in your heart to learn how to direct your prayer in the morning, but need some help to begin doing so, first set your alarm, but also read some helpful books on early morning prayer.

We may not have maids to assign work for the day, but today we have many labor-saving devices that can free us for time in prayer and in the Word of God.

Prudent (v. 16.)

One of the wisest things a woman can learn to do is to say no to new areas of activity that might take her from those things that God would have her doing. Very often these activities are worthwhile; but if they overextend her and keep her from personal time with the Lord and with her family, they are to be turned down rather than taken on.

However, there comes a time when a new "field" is opened to her. She prayerfully considers it, then carefully begins letting it grow into a fruitful activity. The word picture this verse draws is that of an Israelite woman in long-flowing robes looking at a new field on a sunny hillside covered with young grape vines. She asks Jehovah if this is the right field to purchase at that time. She asks if her energies and money should go into this new field which is going to need so much care before it can produce grapes for the table.

The word picture and the setting for a modern woman might be drawn a little differently, yet the question remains the same — and the answer must come from the same source.

An overview of current book and magazine racks will reveal the world's interpretation of this verse. Countless titles centering on the improvement of the body through exercise and diet reveal a preoccupation with the physical aspects of life. Titles and subtitles in the nonfiction section attempt to persuade us that our mind, when properly developed, can conquer our personal world.

Paul, in his writings in 1 Timothy, places the spirit, mind and body into a Christian perspective:

> **But refuse profane and old wives' fables, and exercise thyself rather unto godliness.**
>
> **For bodily exercise profiteth little: but godliness is profitable unto all things, having promise**

of the life that now is, and of that which is to come.

1 Timothy 4:7,8

Many of the mind-improvement books are little more than old wives' tales — empty and without value. After building our spiritual strength through the Word of God and prayer in the Spirit, we will be led of God to choose reading material that will improve our minds. Notice that Paul does not say that physical exercise does no good; rather, he says that it does little in comparison to spiritual exercise.

Faithful (v. 18.)

There is a distinct difference between the satisfaction that comes from doing work "with and for God," and that which comes from doing work in our own power (that which in a way earns us personal credit). There is a momentary satisfaction when we accomplish something that we have selected, managed and worked hard to complete, but the reward ends there. However, when we have committed our work to God, then the benefits from that work leave us with a good taste in our mouth for years to come. (Ps. 103:5.)

"Her lamp goes not out; but it burns on continually through the night." There are some practical reasons for leaving a light on overnight: one is to prevent us from stubbing our toes if we get up during the night; another is to allow a small child to see that all is well in the house. The Hebrews were accustomed to burning lamps all night. A practical reason for this action was to prevent the lamps from having to be relit the next day.

The symbol of lamplight is used many times in the Bible. God's light to us is both His Living Word (Jesus) and His written Word: **Thy word is a lamp unto my feet, and a light unto my path** (Ps. 119:105).

Even as fresh oil was put into the ancient lamps so they would not go out, so our spiritual resources must be renewed. We "store up" these reserves by spending daily time in the Word of God. It will bring understanding and instruction to us and to those around us. The more "oil" (Word) we put in, the brighter our light will burn in our hearts and homes.

As mothers, we have all experienced the night watch, for it is a rare child who does not awaken and need the tender, reassuring care of a mother. We become that strength in the night that our child needs. Our very presence wards off fear and concern in the heart of a small child. Our feet sometimes hit the bedroom floor before he has uttered his second cry. Our thoughts may not have caught up to our bodies at this point, but God has built within us the desire to protect our offspring from darkness and evil of any kind.

As Christians, when times of difficulty come and we are awakened at night, it is time to "turn up the lamp" by speaking the Word of God, praying and singing spiritual songs. Several things happen when we do: 1) God hears our prayers; 2) we hear ourselves, and our hearts are encouraged; and, 3) darkness is dispelled by the light. (See Eph. 5:8-18.)

Ready! (v. 19.)

This woman is in readiness! Her tools are in her hand. Perhaps you have a picture in your mind's eye of a woman you know or have known in the past, and you can imagine her with her tools in her hand. Perhaps it is a lovely neighbor you once knew who greeted you with a garden tool in her hand as she raised up from her rose bed. Maybe it was a grandmother with apron and spoon. Or, perhaps yours is a picture of a mother at a desk with pen in hand.

The picture we have in verse 19 is one of a woman ready to begin a day's work of spinning wool and flax into clothing and household goods. Whether we work in the home exclusively or outside the home as well, it is good to be in readiness to do the work set before us.

Generous (v. 20.)

The Proverbs 31 woman has an abundance. Her hands are full because she has been in preparation. She has more than enough now because she has put her hand to her work and because she serves *El-Shaddai* (the Hebrew word for God which means "the all-sufficient One" or "a God Who is more than enough").

A giving spirit is beautiful. A woman who spends all her time and energy on her family alone and who refuses to share with others is a pathetic figure. Some of us are fortunate enough to have grown up as daughters of giving mothers. Nothing teaches us to give more than that early-set example.

I saw my mother visit the elderly, carry food to the sick and share her love with the brokenhearted. No, this is not a picture of times past. We still have among us the elderly, the poor and the brokenhearted. We may have a family and a job which take up much of our time, but God's instruction to us to care for those in need has not changed. Giving to the poor is so important that when Paul met with the apostles in Jerusalem, they made only one stipulation of him, and that that was to remember the poor. (Gal. 2:10.)

The giver does not look for a reward from those who are the receivers of his gifts. However, there is a reward for those who give.

A number of years ago I helped care for a widow without family who lived across the street from our house. She wanted to remain in her home even though she was in her 80s. I loved her and wanted to help her fulfill her desire. At first it was a visit and a meal that she needed, but before her death the demands became greater and greater. Other than her thank-yous, there certainly was not any tangible reward for me. One day, without my inquiring, the Lord gave me the assurance that because I had willingly helped this elderly lady, I would not be alone without help when I got old.

Prepared (v. 21.)

The Proverbs 31 woman has spent the days before winter producing the clothing that will cover her family in the cold winter months. Some areas of Israel have snowfall, and so the author was writing from experience. As important as the task of dressing the family for the winter months is, this verse has even greater spiritual significance.

The snow speaks of the cold force of evil in the world that a family must face as they leave the safe environment of the home to enter school and work. The godly wife makes sure that her family is not only clothed, but clothed in scarlet. Scarlet is the symbolic color of blood. Her family is covered by the blood of the Savior. She has taught the little ones to trust in God's Son, Jesus, Whose blood was shed on the cross to save us from our sins and to give us eternal life. They do not enter the whirling snow of the world without being clothed in their scarlet garments, for she has taught them about God and covered them with her prayers.

Pure (v. 22.)

The woman of God is not neglectful of herself and her own appearance. She looks to her personal needs. Notice that she wears white linen, both the color and fabric of purity. She has freedom to wear these garments because her life is pure. She also wears the color purple, which in many countries was reserved for royalty and priests. As a woman of Israel, she is certainly the daughter of a chosen generation, even as we are daughters of a chosen generation, for the Word of God says that we are of a royal priesthood. (1 Pet. 2:5-9.) Her desire is to adorn herself and her home in a way that brings honor to her king and to her husband and family.

The New International Version of verse 22 reads: **She makes coverings for her bed....** The work of her hands not only adorns her body but decorates her bed. She knows the importance of the marriage bed. She wants it to be a welcoming place for her husband, a setting of honor and beauty for the sexual union they share. She knows the importance of fidelity in the marriage relationship. (Heb. 13:4.) She is faithful to her husband.

Helpful (v. 23.)

Her husband has a reputation which, in part, is due to his wife. As he goes about the city or community in which he resides, people take notice. Here is a man who has an intelligent, capable and virtuous wife, and it is reflected in his own dress and behavior. He can be confident as he goes about his business "in the gates." In ancient Israel the gates of a city were the place where business was conducted. This man's associates know that he can be trusted. He has a wife who is trustworthy. She contributes to the marriage and does not make financial demands that are beyond their means.

He is not only actively involved in the city's economic, social and spiritual community, he sits among the elders or the leaders. He is an example of the proverb which says, **Whoso findeth a wife findeth a good thing...**(Prov. 18:22.)

Service-minded (v. 24.)

This is a woman who has a part in bringing others into worshipful service to the Lord. She makes fine linen garments and thereby holds up as desirable the role of priest (one who serves God). She leads others into service by helping to stir up their desire to serve the Lord.

Girdles, or sashes, were worn by both men and women and were made of leather or linen. A girdle is symbolic of preparation for battle or active exertion: **Stand therefore, having your loins girt about with truth...**(Eph. 6:14). We are directed to put on the girdle of truth as part of our armor as we withstand the enemy. The woman who is at liberty in the Lord can free others. Through her actions and influence, they can be set free to render the service that the Lord has for them, not what others do or think they should do.

Secure (v. 25.)

As women, we often want to have every little detail nailed down so we can have confidence that all is well. Alas, nailing down details does not assure us of the future. We have planned too many events not to know that things can and do go wrong. Our only hope for the future lies in the promises of God. When we have done all we can, as the Proverbs 31 woman has done, then we can rest secure knowing that God will provide us with what He has promised.

The Proverbs 31 woman wears the clothing of strength and dignity because she has done everything within her power to prepare for her family's future. Now her security and her position are established in God. Newspapers may tell the bad news, but the Bible tells the Good News, and it is this news to which the godly woman and her family subscribe.

Kind (v. 26.)

This is a woman to whom people listen. Why? When she opens her mouth, out if it comes skillful and godly advice that is useful to the hearer.

One of the fruits of the Spirit is kindness. This woman has cultivated that fruit to such a great extent that every time she opens her mouth, kindness comes forth. Her skill in dealing with matters of the family, home and church has been obtained through long hours and days of dedicated service. She is instructed in godly wisdom; therefore, she is qualified and "certified" to counsel and instruct.

Kindness is not an option. It is not an on-again, off-again trait which we can choose or not choose to display. As Christian women, we must have the "law of kindness" continually in our hearts and on our tongues.

Wise (v. 27.)

The wise woman makes choices each hour of each day, choices that are in the best interest of her family — and herself. She chooses constructive tasks. She could spend her time gossiping or shopping, but she continually makes choices that will build up those around her. She makes the most of each and every day — whether it be one of sunshine or of rain. She looks to her household, but she does not rule over its members. She does not have idle time to interfere in the tasks her children are performing. She has trained them, and now she trusts them to carry out their assigned duties.

The wise woman does not need to complain about any situation under which she has to work, for she is content in knowing that she has chosen God's way. She has sought first the kingdom of God and His righteousness and is convinced that all things will be added to her. (Matt. 6:33.)

Blessed (vv. 28,29.)

One of the many rewards for a godly wife and mother is the praise she receives from her family. Her children tell their friends about their mother's goodness; and when they marry and have children, they tell their children. Her name is often on her husband's lips because to him her life has been a book with pages from the Word of God. (1 Pet. 3:1.)

Some of us might say that we hear little of the kind of praise mentioned above. Even if we have heard a little, we would desire to hear more. The praises are nice — they are frosting on the cake — but this woman enjoys praise, she does not depend upon it. She has confidence in God and depends on His praise as she performs those things He has shown her to do.

Reverent (v. 30.)

Most Bible scholars attribute the writing of this proverb to King Solomon; if so, we wonder at what point in his life he drew these conclusions, for he turned away from the teachings of his youth and went after ungodly women and their gods. This passage must have served as indictment to him, if it was written in his youth. If written in his later years, it indicates that he was speaking from a mountain of experience in dealing with the opposite type of woman, for the Bible tells us that...**he had seven hundred wives, princesses, and three hundred concubines: and his wives turned away his heart** (1 Kings 11:3.)

Regardless of who wrote this verse, or when it was written, it remains the truth. The woman who loves the Lord and serves Him from a pure heart will have a lasting treasure. When we begin believing this verse as truth, we will cast away our fears of fading beauty and embrace our relationship with our Lord.

Honored (v. 31.)

The Proverbs 31 woman has not done these works nor developed her character in her own strength, but through the grace of God Whom she worships. The gates often refer to the city itself, and so we we see this woman following after one of her early ancestors, Ruth. Remember what Boaz said to Ruth? **And now, my daughter, fear not; I will do to thee all that thou requirest: for all the city of my people doth know that thou art a virtuous woman** (Ruth 3:11). Honor belongs to the virtuous woman.

As modern women, we too wish to have a prosperous and successful life. How is such a life obtained? By fearing God and worshipfully revering Him. Remember that praise is not necessarily popularity — but even your enemies will recognize that you revere and worship the Lord.

6
According to Thy Word

Mary (Matt. 1:18-25; 2:23; Luke 1:26-56; 2:1-52; Mark 3:31-35; John 2:1-11; 19:26,27.)

As young children, we learn to be obedient to our mothers and fathers and later to teachers and other adults. Although we can be taught from an early age to be obedient to God, true obedience (not mere acquiescence) comes from a heartfelt love for Him and a sincere desire to please Him.

Careful listening to that person whom we love is an important prerequisite to obedience. An example of the importance of listening to the voice of God comes from the book of Exodus. God is speaking to the Israelite nation as they prepare to return to their homeland: **Now, therefore, if ye will obey my voice indeed, and keep my covenant, then ye shall be a peculiar treasure unto me above all people...**(Ex. 19:5). God is telling His people that there is a reward in store for those who hear and obey.

There are many scriptures that demonstrate how women have listened and attended to God's voice. Mary of Bethany (Chapter 7) was one who chose to listen to Jesus; and because she did, He said that she had chosen the good part, one that would not be taken from her. Lydia (Chapter 9) was also obedient. We find Luke saying this of her: **One of those who listened to us was a woman named**

Lydia, from the city of Thyatira, a dealer in fabrics dyed in purple. She was [already] a worshipper of God, and the Lord opened her heart to pay attention to what was said by Paul (Acts 16:14 AMP).

Mary, the mother of Jesus, is an excellent role model in obedience. Not only was she obedient to her God and Savior, but also to those He placed in her life to help her.

Mary

Obedient to God's Word

Mary, a young woman from the Davidic lineage whose foremothers we have studied (Sarah, Ruth, Rahab and Leah), was visited by the angel of the Living God who told her that she was going to bear the Son of God through the power of the Holy Spirit. Starting with this angelic visitation, we begin seeing Mary's life of obedience.

Mary's reply to the angel has rung down through the ages as an example of obedience for all of us: **And Mary said, Behold the handmaid of the Lord; be it unto me according to thy word…**(Luke 1:38).

Mary wanted only what God had ordained for her life. She listened to the angel and, with but one question to help her understand how (not *if*) the conception would take place, she responded in sincere obedience. God had prepared a ready heart for the event that was to take place which had been prophesied by Isaiah 400 years earlier: **Therefore the Lord himself shall give you a sign; Behold, a virgin shall conceive, and bear a son, and shall call his name Immanuel** (Is. 7:14).

Immediately after hearing from the angel, Mary went directly to her older cousin, Elizabeth, whom the angel informed her was also to bear a son. When she arrived at Elizabeth's home, Mary was greeted by her. Elizabeth, who had been barren and was already in her latter years, at that very moment felt life in her womb. She, above all women, now knew that with God all things were possible to one who believes. She recognized that Mary had believed and had received God's Word within her, for she said to Mary: **And blessed is she that believed: for there shall be a performance of those things which were told her from the Lord** (Luke 1:45).

Mary responded to Elizabeth in prophetic song. She revealed her reverence to God by praising Him and giving Him, and Him alone, the credit for the good things that had happened to her. She gave Him honor, for He alone shows mercy throughout the generations to all those who fear Him. (Luke 1:46-55.)

Elizabeth and Mary knew Whom they were obeying — the same God Whom we obey, Whose directives are made known to us through His Word and His Spirit.

It is difficult to even consider a Mary or an Elizabeth who would have refused to accept the honor of bearing Jesus Christ and John the Baptist. Two women — one young and unmarried, the other old and barren, neither having great wealth or position — were chosen by God. He knows hearts and gives His assignments, regardless of how large or small, to those who will yield to Him.

Obedient to God's Chosen Representative

God did not leave to chance the selection of Jesus' earthly father, but chose a just man. Joseph was a man who would provide what the young virgin needed in understanding, care and protection. Mary learned that God would work through Joseph to help her with this revolutionary conception and birth. She knew that he was God's chosen representative to father Jesus during His childhood.

Mary's obedience to God now carried over into her marriage. There are three dramatic situations in which Mary's obedience to Joseph's directions saved the life of the young child, Jesus. Joseph's dreams were his source of direction in all three situations. Hearing God through her own dreams would have required faith from Mary, but an even higher level of faith was required for her to follow the direction of her husband acquired through his dreams.

Jesus was born of Mary in a stable in Bethlehem, as God had foretold through His prophets centuries earlier. The angels gave glory to God, and the shepherds of the hills came to worship the new-born Savior. The Wise Men of the East, who had seen His star, also came to worship the young Jesus. They presented their gifts, and when they left Mary and Joseph, they took a different route back to their homeland. They had been warned in a dream to avoid King Herod, who had requested that they reveal to him the birthplace of the Child.

And when they were departed, behold, the angel of the Lord appeareth to Joseph in a dream, saying, Arise, and take the young child and his mother, and flee into Egypt, and be thou there

until I bring thee word: for Herod will seek the young child to destroy him.

Matthew 2:13

Joseph quickly responded to the warning:

When he arose, he took the young child and his mother by night, and departed into Egypt:

And was there until the death of Herod: that it might be fulfilled which was spoken of the Lord by the prophet, saying, Out of Egypt have I called my son.

Matthew 2:14-15

The couple moved wisely, for in an attempt to destroy the young Child Who was prophesied to be the Ruler of Israel, King Herod ordered the death of all the children two years old and under who were in Bethlehem and "all the coasts thereof."

Mary and Joseph and the Child lived in Egypt until Herod died. Once again Mary was required to follow the directions given to Joseph:

But when Herod was dead, behold an angel of the Lord appeareth in a dream to Joseph in Egypt,

Saying, Arise, and take the young child and his mother, and go into the land of Israel: for they are dead which sought the young child's life.

And he arose, and took the young child and his mother, and came into the land of Israel.

Matthew 2:19-21

While traveling through Israel, Joseph was warned in a third dream about the new ruler in Judea — Archelaus, son of Herod. He was directed to take his wife and the Child to the northern city of Nazareth. It was there in this remote village that Jesus grew up. A disobedient wife might have said to her husband, "Don't you remember the prophecy of Simeon and Anna? How is Jesus going to grow up to be the Redeemer if He is stuck off in this village of Nazareth? I really feel that Jersualem is the place to be." Instead, Mary kept all these things and considered them in her heart.

The only recorded incident that we have of the childhood of Jesus is the account of the trip the family made to Jerusalem in His twelfth year to celebrate the feast of the Passover. At the end of the feast days, the whole company of people from Nazareth started homeward. At the end of the first day's journey, Mary and Joseph discovered that Jesus was not with them. He was not a child who had to be watched, so they had assumed He was with friends and relatives who had made the journey with them. When they found He was not with them, they turned back to Jerusalem to search for Him.

It was three long days before they found Him in the temple, sitting in the middle of the learned men. He was listening to them and also answering their questions. His parents were amazed to find Him there. To them He was still a child and their son. Mary asked why He had stayed behind without telling them, causing them this great concern.

"Why were you searching for me?" he asked. "Didn't you know I had to be in my Father's house?" (Luke 2:49 NIV).

They did not understand His answer, and He did not elaborate. He did something that must have pleased not only Mary and Joseph, but His heavenly

Father as well. He went back home and was obedient to them. ...**But his mother treasured all these things in her heart** (Luke 2:51 NIV.)

After this incident, Joseph is not mentioned again. Most scholars believe he died sometime between the temple passage and the account of Jesus' first miracle. If this is so, Mary lived the next years of her life as a widow.

Obedient to the Savior

Mary and Jesus both attended the wedding at Cana in Galilee. When it became known to Mary that the wine for the wedding guests had run out, she went to Jesus. By this time Mary knew Jesus as her Source. She had pondered the angel's message, as well as the other heavenly signs, for many years as she had watched her Son grow into manhood. When He answered her, not as His mother, but as His disciple, she showed her confidence that His decision in this matter would be the right one. She instructed the servants: ...**Whatsoever he saith unto you, do it** (John 2:5).

It was fitting that Mary, the young woman who had yielded her life to God, should be the one to have a part in her Son's first miracle. As the water was turned to wine that day at the wedding feast, so did the New Wine of Jesus' ministry begin to flow.

Mary learned that all who were obedient could call Him son and brother. It was on a visit with Jesus' brothers that she learned this important lesson:

> **Then His mother and His brothers came, and standing outside they sent word to Him, calling [for] Him.**

> **And a crowd was sitting around Him, and they said to Him, Your mother and Your brothers and Your sisters are outside, asking for You.**
>
> **And He replied, Who are My mother and My brothers?**
>
> **And looking around on those who sat in a circle about Him, He said, See! Here are My mother and My brothers.**
>
> **For whoever does the things God wills is My brother, and sister, and mother!**
>
> Mark 3:31-35 AMP

Mary continued to be obedient to Jesus throughout His ministry. She ministered to Him along with the other women who were His disciples. Her role was different now that His time had come to be revealed as God's only Son. She did not cease to be His mother, now she was His disciple as well.

The elderly prophet, Simeon, had told Mary at the dedication of Jesus that a sword would pierce her heart as her Son revealed the hearts of all men. Time and time again He was misunderstood and evil plots were made against Him. Mary herself did not understand Him at times. Yet the love she had for Him brought her to the foot of the cross at the end of His life on earth.

It was there that John described the last moments of Mary and Jesus at the cross. Standing near the suffering Christ was Mary His mother, Mary the wife of Clopas, Mary Magdala and John. Jesus, seeing His mother and John, said: ..."Dear woman, here is your son," and to the disciple, "Here is your mother"...(John 19:26,27NIV). It was part of His earthly ministry to care for His mother, and now He entrusted her to His beloved disciple. He was bringing all things to completion.

The last and glorious time we hear about Mary is in the first chapter of the book of Acts. She, along with the 120 disciples, waited in the upper room for the Holy Spirit which Jesus had promised to them as He had departed into heaven. (Acts 1:14.) They received the fulfillment of that promise on the day of Pentecost as the Holy Spirit filled them. They then **...began to speak in other tongues, as the Spirit enabled them** (Acts 2:4 NIV). Mary and the other followers now had the enabling power of the Holy Spirit within them. He was the One Who would teach them and help them to be obedient to God's Word.

According to God's Word Today

Obedient to God's Word

We are in a strategic position as women, wives and mothers. No one else has the influence for good and for evil that we do. We have the choice of leading our families in the way of the world or according to the instructions of the Word of God. Obedience to God's Word is not the easiest path; in fact, it may be the most difficult. God may require something of us that goes against the grain of all those around us. Mary was an example of this. She put God's Word above everything else — husband-to-be, family, community, friends and reputation. By being obedient to the Word of God, she had to bear the reproach of others for becoming pregnant before marriage. She could not even defend herself, but had to ponder these things in her heart until the truth was revealed to her.

Mary is revered today, but you can be assured that was not the case in Nazareth 2,000 years ago.

A disobedient woman might have responded to the angel this way: "I am too young. My family is too poor. What will the community think? I am really not ready for this; I am sure you can find someone better qualified."

However, this was not Mary's response. She said, "Be it unto me according to thy word." (Luke 1:38.) Therefore, Mary was blessed above all women. God promises to bless those who receive His Word and meditate on it. (Ps. 1:1-3.) Mary received God's Word first in her spirit and then in her womb. We too must receive the Word of God within us, letting it grow to perfection in our lives.

Mary could respond to the Lord as she did because she belonged to Him. She called herself His handmaid. This is also our primary role. None of the other roles will fall correctly into place until we see ourselves as handmaids of the Lord. (Joel 2:28,29.)

Obedient to God's Chosen Representatives

Although Mary was the mother of Jesus, Lord of the Universe, she was obedient to those whom God put in her life to give her direction. As a young woman, she knew about parental authority. She was also willing to learn from Elizabeth, an older cousin. She agreed to make the difficult journey from Nazareth to Bethlehem, although she was in her last month of pregnancy, in order to register for the tax decreed by Caesar Augustus. After the birth of Jesus, both Mary and Joseph took Him to the temple where they made the acceptable sacrifice for a male child and had Him circumcised in accordance with Jewish law. Finally, Mary was obedient to Joseph as he guided her and the Child safely through the years of Jesus' childhood.

A disobedient woman might have responded differently to her husband's dreams. Her replies might have included: "Let's wait and see if I have the same dream, then we'll go." "Could we wait a few days until I have gone to the river and done the laundry?" "It seems strange to me that God would take this child out of Israel if He is going to be the Messiah." "Let's go to the priests and see if they think we should go to Egypt." "Nazareth is such a remote village, don't you think we would actually be just as safe there?"

Mary's obedience was first to God; however, she knew that He often worked through people whom He placed in her life. That is an important, but difficult, lesson that we all must learn. Have you noticed that God knows when you need to learn this lesson and always provides someone who can teach it to you? Have you also noticed that these people can be some of the most difficult you have ever dealt with? Perhaps the degree of their difficult behavior is proportional to our degree of disobedience.

It is important to recognize people who are really God's representatives in your life. There will be others who claim to have authority over you who do not. It is important to know the scriptures, and to know yourself, so you can respond rightly to those who do have proper authority.

Obedient to Our Savior

Jesus made it clear that if we loved Him we would keep His commandments. He then said that in order to do this, we would receive help from the Comforter — the Spirit of Truth. (John 14:15,16.) It is His Spirit residing in us, and filling us today as He did Mary at Pentecost, that will convict us of sin and of righteousness. It is through the instruction of the Spirit that we can know His will and carry it out in our lives.

As we read the Word of God, the Spirit illumines those verses that are important for us to consider. He warns us of impending temptation, and then convicts us of sin if we did not heed His warning. He leads us to repentance. He comforts us after repentance. Always, always, He leads us into obedience to, and love for, our Savior and Lord. (John 14:26.)

The Spirit of Truth takes us a step farther into obedience by prompting us to tell others about the Lord. (John 14:27.) Even as the disciples were required to testify of the Savior, so must we. If we love Him, we will keep His commandment to tell others about Him so they too can become His disciples. Sex-role stereotyping should never hold us back from obedience to this commandment to witness. It is something that we can do with a whole heart. We can be among that company of women who publish the Word: **The Lord gives the word [of power]; the women who bear and publish (the news) are a great host** (Ps. 68:11 AMP).

7

At His Feet

Mary of Bethany (Luke 10:38-42; John 11:20,28-46; John 12:1-8; Mark 14:8,9.)

Mary of Bethany has given me a better understanding of my role as Christian woman than any other woman of the Bible. Her character has been particularly helpful in showing me how to develop a relationship with Christ.

There are many admirable facets of Mary's personality, but the one that most impresses me is her knowledge of where to go when she had a great need in her life. She did not look first to counseling; she did not seek out a friend; she did not read a book on the subject; but rather, she did the wisest thing of all — she placed herself at the feet of the Master. The three times recorded in the Bible that she does this each have a different application for us, for she had different needs each time.

At His Feet for Instruction

The first time that Mary of Bethany was at the feet of the Master is recorded is Luke 10:38-42:

> Now it came to pass, as they went, that he entered into a certain village: and a certain woman named Martha received him into her house.
>
> And she had a sister called Mary, which also sat at Jesus' feet and heard his word.

But Martha was cumbered about much serving, and came to him, and said, Lord, dost thou not care that my sister hath left me to serve alone? bid her therefore that she help me.

And Jesus answered and said unto her, Martha, Martha, thou art careful and troubled about many things:

But one thing is needful: and Mary hath chosen that good part, which shall not be taken away from her.

Let us visualize the scene. The home of Martha is only a few miles from Jerusalem. It is a place where Jesus feels welcome. He has stopped that day and He is teaching.

As a woman who has prepared some large family meals, it would appear to me that there are a number of people here wanting to hear Jesus's word (for had it been a small group, Martha probably would not have felt "cumbered," or "put upon" in the preparation and service of the food).

Notice also that reference is made to it being Martha's house, not Mary's. (v. 38.) Is Martha the older sister and Mary the younger? It is difficult for us to know for sure, and yet it would appear so.

Are you an "older sister" who feels an obligation, and with it perhaps a resentment, toward those who seem to do less than you? This situation may be in a family setting or even in a church family. You may not be older in actual age, but you can relate to Martha because it seems that you get very little help when you need it the most. At times it does not seem fair that everyone does not take a turn in the kitchen. But it is clear from Jesus' reply to Martha that first things must be put first. Our spiritual appetite is to be given precedence over our physical appetite.

One of the reasons I admire Mary so much is that she receives a commendation from Jesus. It is not only in this passage that He commends her, but in a later episode she also receives His tribute. Jesus makes it clear that being at His feet for instruction is a top priority.

I do not know what the Lord is speaking to you about priorities as a woman (and perhaps as a wife and mother), but I know that He speaks very clearly to me that the study of His Word is a top priority item. Time and time again, I have sought the Lord about situations in my life, and He has brought to mind this verse: **Study to shew thyself approved unto God, a workman that needeth not to be ashamed, rightly dividing the word of truth** (2 Tim. 2:15).

If the word *workman* does not seem appropriate, substitute *worker*, for regardless of our sex, God wants us to study and know His Word. In these times, even as in the time of Mary of Bethany, the Word of God becomes the key to life itself. Jesus did not seem to reserve His teaching for the men, but included Mary in what He called the "good part." (v. 42.)

Notice also in Luke 10:39 that Mary's position denotes more than a casual peek into the Word. She is at the Master's feet. She is as close as she can get. She is not going to miss a word that comes from her Master's lips. She probably has not even seen the furtive looks that Martha has thrown her way as she passes through the room where Jesus is teaching. Mary's eyes have been on the Lord. I believe they are fastened on Him, not staring in a blank pose while thinking of the good meal Martha is going to put on the table, for Mary is taking in the "meat" which Jesus spoke of to His disciples when He talked to the woman at the well. (John 4:32.)

How exciting for us to know that the Holy Spirit has been sent to be our Teacher. (John 14:26.) Like Mary, we can place ourselves at the feet of Jesus; and although He is not with us in physical form, we can receive instruction through the revelation of the Holy Spirit Who resides within us.

Recently, I realized that I needed to set aside more time for prayer and study of the Word of God. I recognized that the only time available to me that would find me at my best physically and mentally was Saturday morning. It was not without a struggle that I gave in to that time period. Saturday morning was *my morning*; it was when I could clean my house, or go to the city and shop, or do nothing at all. I was surprised at how possessive I was of "my" Saturday morning; but I also realized that if I were to follow the instructions which the Lord was speaking to my heart, this was the time to devote to His teaching. As with all sacrifices for the Lord, I knew the benefits would be greater than the sacrifices, and they are already beginning to become mine.

Jesus said to Martha: "But one thing is needful: and Mary hath chosen that good part, which shall not be taken away from her." (v. 42.) The house will receive a cleaning at another time; I might send off for a piece of clothing rather than going out to shop; and there will be other times of recreation — if not, I still have something good that cannot be taken away from me.

At His Feet for Comfort

The second time we find Mary at Jesus' feet is at the death of her brother Lazarus. The death of a loved one is a special time of need when the comfort of the Lord becomes a necessity to bring us beyond our grief; however, the need we have for comfort from Jesus on a daily basis is just as important to our spiritual well-being. Jesus knew this, for when He was getting ready to ascend into heaven to be with the Father, He told His disciples that the Father was sending us the Holy Spirit, the Comforter, Who would teach us all things.

In the same passage, He goes on to say that He also leaves us His peace. (John 14:26,27.) It is the peace and comfort of the Holy Spirit that the person without Christ is missing in this world today, and there is no consolation or comfort that will take their place.

In Chapter 11 of John's Gospel, we read that Lazarus has died and Martha, Mary's sister, has gone to meet Jesus as He nears their village of Bethany. Their brother has now been dead for four days, and Martha and Mary are awaiting the arrival of the Master. Mary has been sitting still in the house, but now her Lord calls for her. Please read the whole chapter, but we will start at verse 29, for it is Mary's response to Jesus that we will be studying:

> **As soon as she heard that** (He was calling for her)**, she arose quickly, and came unto him.**

> **Now Jesus was not yet come into the town, but was in that place where Martha met him.**

The Jews then which were with her in the
house, and comforted her, when they saw Mary,
that she rose up hastily and went out, followed
her, saying, She goeth unto the grave to weep
there.

Then when Mary was come where Jesus was,
and saw him, she fell down at his feet, saying unto
Him, Lord, if thou hadst been here, my brother had
not died.

When Jesus therefore saw her weeping, and
the Jews also weeping which came with her, he
groaned in the spirit, and was troubled,

And said, Where have ye laid him? They
said unto him, Lord, come and see.

Jesus wept.

John 11:29-35

(Of course the account of Lazarus' death does
not end here but just begins, for Jesus raises Lazarus
from the dead and returns him to his sisters Martha
and Mary.)

Martha was the first one to run to Jesus as He
entered Bethany, but we learn that Mary was sitting
still in the house. Some commentators have said that
she was sitting in quiet resignation concerning
Lazarus' death; but, somehow, I picture her being
able to sit quietly until she hears a word from the
Lord. She has been at His feet for instruction so she
knows that He alone has the answer to this problem. I
believe she was waiting for Him to shed His light and
understanding on the situation.

If we would sit quietly and wait for the Lord to
speak to us in the many ways that He is able to do so,
we could find comfort for our sorrow, whether it is

the sorrow of a one-time incident or a long-time sorrow of the heart. If you have a burden, whether it is the loss of a loved one, a rejection by someone close, or a marriage to an unbelieving spouse, there is comfort in Jesus. He has come to bring us deliverance from those sorrows as surely as He delivered Lazarus from the grave.

What is your response to Jesus and His offer of comfort? Have you ever waited longer than necessary, thus spending untold hours in needless hurt and grief? Sometimes we do this because we are out of touch with the Master. It is hard to believe, but we often forget that He told us to come to Him. At other times we feel that we can "handle this one" ourselves, that we do not need to "bother" Him; and yet there is not a scripture to be found anywhere in which the Lord tells us not to "bother" Him when we have a problem and sincerely desire His help. At still other times a self-inflicted martyr's spirit induces us to savor our misery for a while. This is perhaps the most dangerous approach of all, for that time might go on much longer than we first intended. We may set a pattern that will be difficult to escape from even when we have grown tired of it.

Trust is the key to receiving comfort from the Lord, for we can be assured that He will not just pat us on the shoulder and say, "There, there, My dear." Rather, He will bring a solution to our problems and show us the way to walk through our troubles. Mary shows her implicit trust when she tells the Lord that if He had been there her brother would not have died. She had seen death flee at the presence of Jesus, and she knew that all was well when He was on the scene.

If you have a troubled heart, get at the feet of Jesus, for He says to us, **I will not leave you comfortless: I will come to you** (John 14:18). If you feel you do not know how to do this, after having read these scriptures and tried to put them into practice, turn to someone you know who has received comfort from God, and ask them to help you. Because, another way that we receive comfort is through other people.

Mary was being comforted by the Jews as she waited for Jesus. Many times God sends us people who will give us His comfort. We see that this is true, for in 2 Corinthians 1:3,4, we read:

> **Blessed be God, even the Father of our Lord Jesus Christ, the Father of mercies, and the God of all comfort;**

> **Who comforteth us in all our tribulation that we may be able to comfort them which are in any trouble by the comfort wherewith we ourselves are comforted of God.**

Can you imagine the "comforter" and "encourager" that Mary must have become after she had received solace and comfort in Jesus' presence and in His power as He raised her brother from the dead? We become a comforter, as well as the comforted, because it is our scriptural injunction to do so.

At His Feet for Service

The third time Mary was at Jesus' feet is recorded in Mark 14:3-9, Matthew 26:6-13, and finally in John 12:1-7, as follows from *The Amplified Bible:*

> **So six days before the Passover Feast Jesus came to Bethany where Lazarus was, who had died and whom He had raised from the dead.**

So they made Him a supper, and Martha served, but Lazarus was one of those at the table with Him.

Mary took a pound of ointment of pure liquid nard [a rare perfume] that was very expensive, and she poured it on Jesus' feet and wiped them with her hair. And the whole house was filled with the fragrance of the perfume.

But Judas Iscariot, the one of His disciples who was about to betray Him, said,

Why was this perfume not sold for three hundred denarii, and that given to the poor — the destitute?

Now he did not say this because he cared for the poor, but because he was a thief and having the bag [the money box, the purse of the twelve], he took for himself what was put into it — pilfering the collections.

But Jesus said, Let her alone. It was that she might keep it for the time of My preparation for burial — she has kept it that she might have it for the time of My embalming.

You always have the poor with you, but you do not always have Me.

Mary's act was so appropriate and timely that Jesus said (in the Matthew and Mark versions of this story) that wherever the Gospel was preached this service would be a memorial to her. It is not that we expect every service we perform for Christ to be as notable as this one; but we can learn a great deal from this demonstration of service, for it was conceived in this woman through a great sensitivity of her spirit. When the others were saying "No, no" to Jesus' proclamation of His coming death, she had an ear that listened and a heart that obeyed.

Gordon Lindsay in his *Life of Christ Series,* says: "Mary alone seemed to understand what Jesus meant when He spoke about His death, burial and resurrection. Nor was Mary present with the other women who went to embalm the Lord. She knew that the one who had raised her bother Lazarus from the dead would not remain in the tomb. He was the resurrection and the life, and death could not hold him."[1]

It is the kind of attitude that Mary had toward serving Jesus that will bring us His commendation. Our service may be small and may go unnoted while we are here on this earth, yet if it is something done in tune with the leading of the Holy Spirit, it will be recognized by Jesus. Mary could not have sensed that this was the right thing to do if she had not known Jesus intimately, and this intimacy came by being at His feet at other times. She knew her Lord, and she knew how to serve Him.

In verse 3, we notice that something happened immediately after Mary poured the perfume upon Jesus' feet — the whole house was filled with the fragrance of the perfume. As women, we enjoy fragrance so much that we buy sprays and lotions for ourselves and our loved ones. We place potpourri, scented candles and flowers around our homes. In Proverbs 27:9, we read that oil and perfume rejoice the heart. It is a marvelous revelation to know that as we serve Jesus, our houses, like Martha's, will be filled with a supernatural fragrance.

---

[1] Gordon Lindsay, *Life of Christ Series,* "Christ Teaches the Apostles," Vol. XII (Dallas: Christ for the Nations, 1971) p. 32.

I love to think about Mary's decision to take this very costly fragrance and lavish it upon the feet of Jesus (and upon His head, as noted in Matthew's version). Was this ointment being saved for a family burial? Was it something Mary herself had saved to purchase? Was it purchased days or weeks ahead of time for the express purpose of anointing Jesus; or did she simply use this treasure on the appointed day when Jesus came to their village to eat with them? Although it may have been a spontaneous response to all the things Mary had heard Jesus saying about His impending death, I like to think that she had spent some time in anticipation and excitement thinking about the way she could best serve her Master.

The shocked reaction of those at the table indicates that Mary had kept her secret well. How important this is, for at times to tell someone of a service we are about to perform takes away from the pleasure we receive from performing it; indeed, it may even cancel the very effect that is to take place.

Mary broke the traditions of the Jews as she wiped Jesus' feet with her hair. She must have entered the room with her hair unbound, or else have unbound it as she sat at His feet. Either way, it was not proper for a Jewish woman to do so. Not only did her hair flow down her back, but she actually used it as a towel to wipe the excess perfumed oil which dripped from Jesus' feet. This could have easily been interpreted by some at the table (and probably was) as a sensual, overly familiar act. But Jesus knew Mary's heart and was touched by the purity of her devotion.

Mary was willing to risk the reproach of those around her who would not understand her motives. It may not be often that we are called to violate the sanctions of society in order to serve Jesus, but when we are, can we do it boldly and without embarrassment? Do we fashion our service by the mores of our times or by the Word of God?

Judas hypocritically asked why the perfume had not been sold and the money spent on the poor. But Jesus indicated that there would be ample time to give to the poor after His death. Mary's sacrifice was timely. It was the priority of the hour. Giving unto the Lord is one of the most satisfying acts which we as women can perform. We too can experience the exultation and excitement of Mary as we give generously of all we have in time, money and goods; but even more so as we lavishly give Him the praise and adoration He desires.

A New Application: At His Feet

I do not believe it is difficult for a sincere, Christian woman to put into practice the example given us by Mary of Bethany in her relationship to Christ. We soon learn that our Lord is a kind and gentle Instructor, One Who comforts us in our sorrows and appreciates our service. The continuous faithfulness of the Lord to us in every circumstance of life paves the way for our trust. After all, it is a perfect Savior at Whose feet we sit.

A new and more demanding application of Mary's principles would be in our relationship to our husbands. I believe we women can benefit greatly by going to our *own* husbands for instruction, comfort and service. If this sounds ridiculous to you, it is because it runs contrary to almost everything that is written in secular literature today. "At His feet" does not mean underneath His feet. Mary's posture was an attitude as much as a position. It was based on love and respect, not fear and subservience.

Time and time again we see, in the Bible, the bride likened to the Church, and the groom to Christ. (Please read Ephesians 5:22-33 before continuing this chapter.) Realize that a great deal is also required of the husband, but we can only learn what God requires of us as wives (or wives-to-be).

At his Feet for Instruction

Perhaps believing that their husbands have the answers to life's problems, both large and small, comes easy for some women; however, I would venture a guess that a great many women (like me) have grown up thinking that we wives have the better answer — or certainly ones just as good.

It took a great deal of revelation from the Word of God, as well as anointed teaching, before I came to understand that my husband could instruct me in the ways of the Lord, even if I spent more time in the Word and in prayer than he did. When I began obeying the Word, these principles began to work and I experienced the benefits of godly advice from my husband's lips. That change brought a great freedom for me, for up until that time I had felt that I was the sole guide in the Christian faith in our family, which included four adolescent children. My coming to my husband and expecting the Lord to speak to me through him not only freed me, it also brought him a great deal of respect and esteem as well.

It took a while to get the children to go to their father for instruction because of the years they had come to me, but when they did, the results were in great benefits to their lives. It was not that I did not offer suggestions for any solution, but I did not insist on my own way; instead, I trusted that if what I was suggesting had merit, the Lord would see that it was incorporated into the decision. Many times it was.

The more I went to my husband for instruction, the more responsibility he felt to give godly advice. At times, husbands will refuse that responsibility and be unwilling to give instruction. It is then time to back off. Certain things may need immediate attention, but it is important to make your request and then leave it with your husband. It may be months before he gives you an answer, but giving him time leaves the responsibility with him rather than having it revert to you.

Perhaps you are wondering just what kind of instruction you can receive from your husband. I believe you can receive instruction in every area of your life. Just as it takes a period of time for most people to submit all areas of their lives to Jesus' direction, so it takes a period of time to learn to bring all areas of your life to your husband. I am not implying that wives should run to their husbands with every little detail of life, for it is not necessary to bring those areas in which agreement already exists.

Each couple will find that there are different areas in their lives that need to be dealt with through instruction. For example, I find that my husband has given me wise instruction in the following areas: 1) how to relate to our grown children; 2) how to deal with authority figures; 3) how to dress in a way that is comfortable for me, yet pleasing to him; and, 4) how to test the spirits.

Many times as my husband was instructing me in these areas, my feelings would be hurt because they were areas of difficulty in which I could not always see that I was wrong. I often took his instruction as criticism, at first. Later, I saw that it was actually instruction, that he was seeing things about me that I was not able to perceive about myself. Granted, at times our husbands do not speak as gently while giving instruction as they should. At such times, we must look to God for grace and comfort.

I would have to add that a wife often brings instruction to her husband, for it is by the way she conducts her life — her lifestyle — that he learns from her. (1 Pet. 3:1.) For example, my husband began walking in divine health because he saw that it was through applying biblical principles of divine health and healing that I was able to walk in continual health. I have also, with the leading of the Holy Spirit, been able to instruct my husband in certain truths. Unfortunately, there were other times when I instructed him and realized afterwards that my instruction was inappropriate.

At his Feet for Comfort

Many Christian and secular psychologists are convinced that young women, as well as older women, have a need for the love of a father. Lack of such love has caused many a young woman to turn to unhealthy relationships with men, in search of fulfillment of this deepfelt need. One aspect of fatherly love is the ability to comfort. In the first part of this chapter, we looked at a scripture which spoke of God as "the God of all comfort." (2 Cor. 1:3.) If we are mature in our Christian walk, we will seek comfort from God as soon as it is needed. However, often when we are young in Christ, we do not recognize the total and all-available quality of our heavenly Father's love.

We often need to look for comfort from others, even as we sought comfort from our parents when we were children. If you did not have parents who were able or willing to comfort you in the way you desired, be assured that your heavenly Father is never lacking in this quality.

We can usually find comfort in reading the Word of God, in talking to the Father or from experiencing the healing presence of the Holy Spirit within us. However, there are times when we need other members of the Body of Christ to bring us comfort: **And whether one member suffer, all the members suffer with it; or one member be honoured, all the members rejoice with it** (1 Cor. 12:26). It is important not to confuse our occasional desire for agreement on how we have been wronged with a genuine need for comfort. Those who comfort do not always need to know what the source of our hurt is in order to administer comfort. Indeed, many times the details are better left unspoken.

God does use others, including our husbands, to bring us comfort. This ability that God has given my husband really was brought home to me a couple of years ago when I had experienced an extremely stressful day. I had made it a point not to bother my husband about every little problem having to do with my teaching job. However, one evening I came home from work and went to bed troubled in spirit. In the middle of the night I suddenly awoke in great anxiety. I turned to the Lord for comfort and began praying, but it was through my husband that the Lord worked to comfort me. And a great comfort it was too, for I had been trying to handle things in the same way he did. That night he took me in his arms and I was enfolded and warmed as I drifted off to sleep thinking of the goodness of the Father and my husband.

During the next few days, I was reminded of several wonderful scriptures about our being kept "in the bosom of the Lord." This is important for us to see, because we cannot spend all our time enfolded in someone else's bosom. However, we can be in the Father's bosom at all times when we are in Christ, for we read: **No man hath seen God at any time; the only begotten Son, which is in the bosom of the Father, he hath declared him** (John 1:18).

Intimacy such as this does not come in a few hours or days; neither does intimacy with the Father come in a few seconds of hurried prayer. As we continuously seek His presence in His Word and in prayer, we can continually find the love and comfort that has already been made available to us. In the same way, we must take the time to come into the intimacy and comfort of our husband's bosom.

At his Feet for Service

In John 12:1-7 Mary of Bethany was at Jesus' feet for an express purpose, and that was to serve Him and to anoint His body for burial.

I think it is important here to distinguish between the different types of servitude. Mary is not a slave out of obligation, but instead a trusted friend who chooses to serve because it is the sincere desire of her heart to do so. She is not being forced to perform this service, and indeed the others present are offended by the lavishness of her service. She is sensitive to her Lord alone and does what is right at the moment — thus should our service be to our husbands.

Service does not imply a prescribed set of duties that must be performed routinely, but a sensitivity of spirit that allows us to be the helpmate that God created woman to be in the beginning when He formed Eve from Adam's side and brought her to him. (Gen. 2:18-25.)

As I observe Mary of Bethany at the feet of Jesus, I see one other very important position and that is by His side when others are in opposition to Him. I am sure that at Martha's house that day there were devoted followers of Christ, but on the issue of His death they were in opposition to their Lord.

Our husbands face much opposition from others in their lives and we, like Mary, can serve them in the deepest sense by being on their side during times of opposition. That does not mean that we have to fight their battles for them, but it does mean that we listen to them and let them know that we support them fully. We may not fully understand what the real problem is, as I am sure Mary did not fully understand the meaning of Christ's death and resurrection, but it does mean that we serve them fully, as Mary served Jesus in such a way that showed that she was with Him in this most challenging of times.

I remember one particularly difficult winter when my husband, in his role as high school basketball coach, was facing great opposition from certain individuals. This opposition took the form of verbal abuse, threatening phone calls and minor damage to our home. Through that winter, the way I could best serve my husband was to let him know that I approved of him and believed in him fully. I had only to support him through prayer and my presence at the games.

As I spent time in prayer, the verse the Lord gave me for that situation was: **Fear not; [there is nothing to fear] for I am with you; do not look around you in terror and be dismayed, for I am your God. I will strengthen and harden you [to difficulties]; yes, I will help you; yes, I will hold you up and retain you with My victorious right hand of rightness and justice** (Is. 41:10 AMP).

We can learn to give anointed service to our husbands through Mary's example.

8

Worship in Spirit and Truth

The Samaritan Woman (John 4:1-43.)

Jesus gives drink to the thirsty today even as He did when He walked the roads of Samaria on that day He talked with a thirsty woman at Jacob's well.

Much has been said about the reputation of the Samaritan woman, but since Jesus did not condemn her, this can hardly be the issue. Many have found her remarks to be sly and defensive, but Jesus could have sought out a Pharisee if He had been looking to bring unto Himself someone with those characteristics. Does the Bible say that **...he must needs go through Samaria...**(v. 4) because He knew there was one there who thirsted for Him? Did He reveal Himself so openly to this particular woman because He saw within her a heart that sought God?

Jesus still seeks those today who will worship Him **...in spirit and in truth** (v. 24.) Those who ask, seek and knock are still the ones who receive from God. (Luke 11:10.)

The Samaritan Woman

A Thirsty Woman Meets Jesus

Jesus was very tired the day that He sat down by Jacob's well. He knew it was wise to leave Judea and go back to His home territory of Galilee. The Pharisees had learned that He was gaining more disciples than John the Baptist and that His disciples had now started to baptize. Unlike most Jews, He chose to go to Galilee by passing through Samaria rather than skirting around it. He chose to take this direct route, a route that was normally avoided by the Jews because of their long-held hatred of the Samaritans.

Jesus had not been sitting in the heat of the noonday sun for long when a woman approached the well. An ordinary Hebrew man might have thought: "Oh, no, just when I had the privacy to speak with My Father. I think I'll just ignore her and she won't dare approach me, a Jew." But, of course, that was not Jesus' way. He did not turn His head and ignore the woman as she approached with her water pot.

Many have felt that this woman's reputation was so notorious that she was forced to come to the well at noon, a time when no other women would be around. However, it would have been difficult in those days for a woman to carry out her household duties without coming into contact with other women. Certainly trips to the marketplace and the well were daily necessities. Could it have been that she had just run out of water? Or had she run out of the will to govern her own life? Had the Spirit of God drawn her to the well that day? Jesus Himself said that no one can come to Him unless the Father draws him. (John 6:44.) Life-changing encounters with Jesus are never by chance.

The Samaritan woman was curious. She had noticed the figure of the man as she had neared the well and had noted that He was a Jew. She wondered what this man with the peaceful countenance would do when she came near Him. She watched Him out of the corner of her eye. He did not avert His eyes but looked directly at her. This surprised and delighted her; obviously this was not one who would distainfully move away as she moved closer to lower the bucket into the well.

Jesus asked her for a drink. Slowly continuing to draw the water from the deep well, she asked Him: "How is it that You, being a Jew, ask me, a Samaritan woman, for a drink?" (v. 9.) They both knew that a religious Jew would not speak to a Samaritan because of the long-standing animosity between the two peoples. For Jesus, a man, to speak to a woman in this kind of situation was another break with tradition. What was behind this man's request? Certainly He was not an ordinary man, she thought.

> **Jesus answered her, If you had only known and had recognized God's gift, and Who this is that is saying to you, Give Me a drink, you would have asked Him instead and He would have given you living water.**
>
> **John 4:10** AMP

Something began stirring deep within her. What kind of man was this? He did not speak like any man she knew. She needed to find out Who He was, and why He was talking to her in this manner:

> **She said to Him, Sir, You have nothing to draw with (no draw-bucket) and the well is deep; how then can You provide living water? — Where do You get Your living water?**
>
> **John 4:11** AMP

Somehow she knew that He could explain away the physical limitations. She was struggling now, for she had lived so long in her dreary circumstances.

She had been rejected by those she loved. Could she trust this man to tell her the truth?

> **Are You greater than and superior to our ancestor Jacob, who gave us this well, and who used to drink from it himself, and his sons and his cattle also?**
>
> John 4:12 AMP

In order to produce this living water, this young Jew would have to be even greater than Jacob whose greatness was known from times past. "A gift from God," she thought. "Oh, how I need a gift from God right now."

> **Jesus answered her, All who drink of this water will be thirsty again.**
>
> **But whoever takes a drink of the water that I will give him shall never, no never, be thirsty any more. But the water that I will give him shall become a spring of water welling up (flowing, bubbling) continually within him unto (into, for) eternal life.**
>
> John 4:13,14 AMP

All the longing of her soul rose up within her as she said to Him: "Give me a drink of this water!" (v. 15.) She had been thirsty all her life. She had tried to satisfy her own thirst, but nothing had really quenched it. Now here was One Who was willing to give her a drink that would satisfy that longing, not just for the moment but for eternity.

God Seeks True Worshippers

Jesus told the woman to go call her husband and then come back to the well.

> **The woman answered, I have no husband. Jesus said to her, You have spoken truly in saying, I have no husband.**
>
> **For you have had five husbands; but the man you are now living with is not your husband. In this you have spoken truly.**
>
> John 4:17,18 AMP

The hot Samaritan sun shone high in the sky but there was a new light shining, and it was in her very being. "Sir," she said respectfully, her eyes searching His face for more clues of His identity. "I see that You are a prophet." (v. 19.)

Here was One like the scriptures spoke of — One Who had knowledge from God of secret things. "Here is the One Who will explain this contradiction to me," she thought. She said to Him:

> **Our forefathers worshipped on this mountain, but you [Jews] say that Jerusalem is the place where it is necessary and proper to worship.**
>
> John 4:20 AMP

Jesus answered her in a way that had not yet been revealed to many. He said, "The day is coming when people will not worship merely in a place, but in a new manner." (vv. 21,22.)

Now her heart beat loudly within her, for she began feeling the very presence of God at this well of Jacob, the patriarch. This living water was filling the crevices of her empty soul, running into the corners of her heart and mind as He continued pouring His words upon her:

> **A time will come, however, indeed it is already here, when the true (genuine) worshippers**

will worship the Father in spirit and in truth (reality); for the Father is seeking just such people as these as His worshippers.

God is a Spirit (a spiritual Being) and those who worship Him must worship Him in spirit and in truth (reality).

John 4:23,24 AMP

Surely only the One Who was yet to come could help her comprehend what this man was saying. Oh, how she desired to be one of those who were sought by God to worship Him in this new way of spirit and truth. "It is the Messiah Who will reveal all things to us when He comes," she said. (v. 25.)

Jesus answered her, "I am He." (v. 26.)

This lowly Samaritan woman had been given His undivided attention as He revealed to her — a woman His own disciples would not have bothered with — His identity which had been hidden from the wisest of men. Indeed, He does seek those who will worship Him in spirit and in truth.

Jesus Desires Disciples to Go Forth

The disciples returned from the town where they had bought food for a meal. When they saw Jesus talking to a Samaritan woman, who appeared to them to be married, they were astonished. But they did not question Him about her. They knew from experience that if they accused Him of doing something they thought was not right, He would show them to be the ones who needed to change. They thought they would just let this interlude pass and get on with the meal they were so hungrily awaiting.

At their arrival, the woman left her water pot and returned to the town. Her errand was forgotten in the wonder of meeting the Messiah. She raced to the town and, as she encountered the men there, she began eagerly sharing her experience with Jesus.

"He told me everything I have ever done," she said. "Is this not the Messiah?" (v. 29.) She would not withhold this tremendous gift. It began flowing from her as He had said it would; first streams, then rivers began tumbling from her lips. This was not just for her, it was for all. She knew the scriptures well enough to know that the Living Water the Messiah offered was for everyone. Her generous heart had been opened, and she would not stop telling what she had experienced with Him.

In the meantime, the disciples were urging Jesus to eat the food they had brought. He perceived that they had missed the point of the encounter with the woman. They had their minds on the meal and their hearts centered on the traditions of their fathers which forbade contact with the Samaritan people.

Jesus said to them, "I have food you don't know about." (v. 32.)

Hmmmm, they pondered. Had the woman given Him something to eat? Would He really *eat* food given to Him by a Samaritan woman? Certainly He had not been *that* hungry. Picking grain in the field on the Sabbath was one thing, but...no, surely not.... Had someone else brought Him something to eat?

Their understanding was still dull.

**Jesus said to them, My food (nourishment)
is to do the will (pleasure) of Him Who sent Me**

and to accomplish and completely finish His work.

John 4:34 AMP

He explained to them that the will of the Father was to give the Water of Life to thirsty souls. It was to look at the need of a person and not his race, nor his rank, nor his reputation. "The fields are white for harvesting," He said. He was telling them what He would say again just before He ascended into heaven. They were to preach the Gospel to everyone. It was to be first priority; and if they would share the Bread of Life with others, they too would have the nourishment they needed.

Meanwhile, the Samaritans from the town who believed the woman came to Jacob's well to see the One she spoke about. They urged Him to stay with them. Jesus stayed there two days, and many believed His testimony for themselves.

Worshipping in Spirit and Truth Today

Thirsty Women Meet Jesus

The Samaritan woman did not even know it was God she thirsted for. She only knew that she had not experienced true satisfaction in life. Her five marriages had dissolved, and now she was living with a man to whom she was not married. Since men were the only ones permitted to obtain divorces at that time, it is difficult to know what her part was in the marital rifts. We cannot lay blame on her, nor can we absolve her. It is not really for us to decide the issue anyway, for the Master has already decided. He offered Himself to her, for He knew that He was what she really thirsted for.

She was obviously a curious woman, for she eagerly engaged in conversation with Jesus. If she had been dull of mind and spirit, she would have grunted a yes or no to His comments. Instead, she pursued them. Jesus must have enjoyed His time with her. It was not often that the throngs of people were not pressing in on Him. Now He had the time and privacy to address this woman in a deep and personal way. He did not see her as a woman with multiple husbands, but as a woman in need of salvation.

When Jesus spoke with her, He forever resolved the issue of the type of person who could come into the Kingdom of God. We sometimes forget the lesson He taught His disciples so many years ago — He gives Living Water to any who thirst. (John 7:37,38.)

It is important today to remember that there is no woman who is beyond receiving from Him. Sometimes we forget this fact when we consider those against whom we have formed barriers.

The two types of women who are often the hardest to witness to are the ones at each end of the social spectrum — those who are morally destitute, and those who appear to be materially prosperous. Somehow we begin thinking that the destitute woman's problems are too serious to be solved. When we look at the prosperous woman, we tend to think that she has no needs, no problems to be resolved. Both responses are wrong.

Living Water is sufficient to bring new life to the destitute and the affluent. If the woman who appears to "have it all" has not had a drink of the Living Water, she really does not have life at all.

There are many thirsty women today who need Jesus.

God Seeks True Worshippers

We can be assured that before we ever seek God, He is seeking us, even as He loved us before we ever loved Him. Certainly this woman knew that there was nothing she could do on her own to please God. She knew the rules that the Jews and the Samaritans imposed, and she knew that she had hopelessly failed to keep them.

Jesus gave this curiosity-seeker something to think about when He described the true worshipper. "God is a Spirit," He said, "and those who worship Him must worship Him in spirit and in truth." What does this mean? It was certainly something new for the woman at the well, for the Samaritans said that it was on Mt. Gerizim and the Jews said that it was in Jerusalem that one had to worship God. Some would say today, "Surely, it is in *our* church that God must be worshipped."

Jesus was beginning to reveal to this woman what the New Covenant would be like. The true worshippers would worship God in spirit and in truth. God is still seeking such worshippers. He equips us for this worship. He gives His Spirit to each and every believer; and when Jesus ascended to the Father, He sent the Holy Spirit to empower us. He gave us Himself, which is Truth, and His Word, which is Truth. If it is the desire of our heart to worship Him in spirit and in truth, He will show us how.

Jesus Sends Us Forth

Jesus had not even given His great commission to the Church when He met the Samaritan woman, yet she took Him so seriously that she ran forth from Him to tell everyone that the Messiah had come. (Mark 16:15; Acts 1:8.) Today we do have the commission to go forth and tell people about Jesus the Savior. In order to do that on a regular basis, we must go to the Lord and His Word.

Water that is recirculated over and over without a fresh source becomes stagnant. So it is with us. This is what Jesus was trying to show the woman and His disciples. The pleasures of this life will never satisfy our thirst. The psalmist David said of the righteous: "God shall make them drink of the rivers of His pleasures for in Him is the fountain of life." (Ps. 36:8.) It is essential to drink from Him.

Mountain Stream

Be as the mountain stream;
It moves quickly and is fresh
and clean.
As it reaches the bottom, it spills over
rocks to form a waterfall.
Rainbows are formed in the sparkling
water and prisms of light dance in it.
Let rainbows show forth in your life
so people may see the beauty of
My life in you.

Know that the mountain stream looks
not to the stagnant pool to renew itself
but begins again at the
top of the mountain.
Come to the top of the mountain for
your fresh supply from Me.

9
An Opened Heart

Lydia (Acts 16)

Lydia is often esteemed because of her generous hospitality to Paul and to others in the early Church. She was a businesswoman — a seller of purple cloth — and she spent her income wisely. Another quality of Lydia, which is equally to be desired, is her open heartedness. Without an open heart, she would not have been the first European convert to Christ, nor would she have helped build the church at Philippi which Paul called his "joy and crown." (Phil. 4:1.) A heart opened by God is the first prerequisite for spiritual growth.

Paul, on his second missionary journey, was building and establishing churches by the leading of the Holy Spirit. He found that the Spirit forbade him to go into certain territories. Being obedient to this leading, he, Silas and Timothy avoided passing through those areas. Instead, they went down to Troas: **[There] a vision appeared to Paul in the night: a man from Macedonia stood pleading with him and saying, Come over to Macedonia and help us!** (Acts 16:9 AMP). Paul understood from this vision that Macedonia was where they were to preach the Gospel.

Paul and the other men sailed to Philippi, in that day the chief city of Macedonia, a Roman colony.

They stayed a few days in the city and on the Sabbath went to the river to look for the prayer meeting of the faithful. Paul and his companions knew that when there was no Jewish synagogue in a city, the Jews of that area met by the banks of the river. This was a practice that had its roots in the time they were driven from their homeland into other countries of the world: **By the rivers of Babylon, there we sat down, yea, we wept, when we remembered Zion** (Ps. 137:1).

A Woman of Prayer

And on the Sabbath day we went outside the [city's] gate to the bank of the river, where we supposed there was [an accustomed] place of prayer, and we sat down and addressed the women who had assembled there (Acts 16:13 AMP).

The fact that Paul found only women at prayer did not deter him from preaching. Whether it was their prayer that led Paul to the area to give them the spiritual help they desired, we do not know. It would not be presumptuous to believe this was the case because it was to the women that Paul first preached the message of Christ in that part of the world. Women of prayer can change the course of history.

There was a special woman praying at the riverside that day: **One of those who listened to us was a woman named Lydia, from the city of Thyatira, a dealer in fabrics dyed in purple. She was [already] a worshipper of God, and the Lord opened her heart to pay attention to what was said by Paul** (Acts 16:14 AMP).

There were a number of women praying on that Sabbath day, and yet one woman is singled out by Luke as he records the Acts of the Apostles. Was Lydia's position and wealth the factor that caused her to be mentioned in the Word of God? Her career and position in life were part of her, and therefore bore mention; but Paul did not seek to preach to either those of high position or to those of low position — he sought all those who would listen and pay attention.

A Woman Who Listened

Careful listening is an important prerequisite to obedience. It is attending to the words that we hear spoken to us that leads us into obedience.

The importance of hearing God's voice is made clear to us when we read how God talked to the children of Israel as they prepared to return to their homeland: **Now therefore, if ye will obey my voice indeed, and keep my covenant, then ye shall be a peculiar treasure unto me above all people...**(Ex. 19:5). Notice that God said, "If you will obey My voice, you will be a treasure to Me." It takes an open ear, as well as an open heart, to hear the Lord. For faith comes by hearing, and hearing by the Word of God. (Rom. 10:17.)

Lydia had to be in the position of hearing the Word of God before she could receive salvation. The choice she made to assemble with the women on the riverbank for prayer was what allowed her to hear God's words through Paul. God had opened the heart of this Gentile woman to worship Him, and now again He opens her heart to pay attention to the message of Christ. The teachings of Jesus point out that no man (or woman) can come to Him unless he (or she) is drawn by the Father. (John 6:44.) Even as Paul was led to Macedonia by the Spirit, so was Lydia drawn to Christ by God's Spirit.

A Woman of Industry

Lydia was a seller of purple cloth. She was a businesswoman. This was part of who she was, even as Priscilla was a craftswoman. God is not a respecter of persons. (Acts 10:34.) He opened the heart of this Gentile woman. He meets women where they are, regardless of their role in life. He draws princesses, harlots, housewives and career women to Him because He loves them all.

In that first century, status was attached to those who sold purple cloth. Only the rich could afford fabrics dyed in a costly process which involved the extracting of dye from tiny shellfish. It was a prestigious and profitable business, and surely brought Lydia in contact with the wealthy of the Macedonian region.

Edith Deen, in her book, *All the Women of the Bible*, makes this comment about Lydia's name: "The old kingdom of Lydia, of which Croesus was the last king, was the region in Asia Minor from which Lydia had come. It had five large cities, Ephesus, Smyrna, Sardis, Philadelphia, and Thyatira, all located on or near the chief rivers and connected with the coastal cities by good roads. The Lydian market, as it was called, had enjoyed for generations a wide and valuable trade throughout the Graeco-Roman world. This woman evidently was so closely allied with her old environment of Lydia that her personal name was actually that of her native province."[1]

Imagine how successful and effective a salesperson Lydia must have been for her name to be one and the same as the province made famous by the sale of the costly purple goods. Evidently, however, wealth and position were not enough for Lydia, even as it is not enough for those of high economic status today (whether they know it or not). She had a heart that could not be fed with material wealth. The One True God Who had opened her heart to worship Him, also opened her heart to worship Christ.

A Woman of Action

Many hear and walk away. Lydia decided to put action to her faith. She did this by hearing Paul's words and then following his instructions to be baptized. Not only was she baptized, but her whole household was baptized also. Some, or even all, of her household may have been there that day on the riverbank. Maybe others heard and believed after Paul came to visit in the home. Perhaps Lydia herself led them to Christ.

We do not know whether Lydia's household consisted of relatives or household workers, children or adults. A husband is not mentioned, so Lydia either was a widow or had never been married. Like many women today, she was responsible for a household. Lydia not only helped meet their material needs, but she helped meet their spiritual needs as well. She was an unmarried Proverbs 31 woman!

---

[1]Edith Deen, *All the Women of the Bible* (New York: Harper & Brothers, 1955) pp. 221-222.

Lydia was willing to be judged faithful: **And when she was baptized along with her household, she earnestly entreated us, saying, If in your opinion I am one really convinced [that Jesus is the Messiah and the Author of salvation], and that I will be faithful to the Lord, come to my house and stay. And she induced us [to do it]** (Acts 16:15 AMP).

Here was a woman sensitive enough to know that Paul could not stay just anywhere. He needed a special place to live. She discerned the mission of this man. For him to bring the Gospel to this pagan people with their many gods, he had to be with those he could trust. Lydia wanted to be counted in that number of the faithful. She desired the privilege of having these men of God stay in her household. She wanted to bless them, but she knew also that as she did, her whole household would be blessed. She was like the Shunammite woman who made a comfortable room for the prophet Elisha so he could have a place to rest when he passed through the region where she lived. (2 Kings 4:8-10.)

Not only did Lydia ask Paul and his companions to stay in her home, but she "induced" them to do so. She entreated them, letting them know what a privilege it would be for her. Her invitation was given out of a sincere desire to open her home to the men who had brought her to the saving knowledge of Jesus Christ. She, like so many of the women in the Bible, promoted the Gospel through hospitality.

A Woman of Courage in Time of Trial

After the first Sabbath meeting, Paul and the other believers continued to go to the riverbank for

Sabbath prayer, since there was no synagogue in Philippi.

One day as they walked to the place of prayer, they encountered one of the many forces of darkness that were present in that city. A young woman slave was possessed of a spirit of divination which recognized who the group was and Whom they served. When the girl saw Paul and his friends, the spirit screamed through her: ...**These men are the servants of the Most High God! They announce to you the way of salvation!** (Acts 16:17 AMP).

Paul tried to ignore her as he quietly went about establishing his work in the city. Finally, after many days, he tired of having his mission announced from such a source. He commanded the demon spirit of divination to come out of the girl in the name of Jesus. It left her, and with it went her owners' source of income, for they had used her to tell fortunes. In their anger, the girl's masters dragged Paul and Silas before the authorities located in the marketplace. The men of God were then stripped, beaten and thrown in jail by order of the rulers.

The episode of the young girl with the spirit of divination did not end with Paul's imprisonment. God turned the prison experience into something good. As Paul and Silas sang praises to God in the midnight hour in the depths of their jail cell, God caused an earthquake that loosened their prison chains. The jailer, terrified that his prisoners had gone free, was overcome with fear. When Paul and Silas assured him that they had not escaped, the jailer fell down before them in repentance. Not only did they help save his natural life, but more importantly they told him to believe in the Lord Jesus for eternal life. The jailer and his entire family believed and were baptized. (Acts 16:22-39.)

The jailer bathed the men's wounds and fed them. When they were released, Paul and Silas went directly to Lydia's house to meet the believers who were gathered there. (v. 40.)

Lydia was a model hostess. She did not open her house only when times were good, but even in time of trial. She had made the decision that regardless of the civil authorities' view of her alliance with Paul, she would not shun her reponsibility. It would have been praiseworthy of her to have opened her home in a city of a Christian majority; but when, in the midst of this pagan city, she showed hospitality to these men of God, she marked herself as a martyr. Lydia was not opening her home to the "citizens of the year," for when the authorities released Paul and Silas they asked them to leave the city.

The encouragement that Lydia and the others received from Paul and Silas that day must have spurred them onward, for from this small nucleus was born the church that Paul so lovingly addressed in his letter to the Philippians.

Opened Hearts Today

The lives of women in the Bible have given us insight into the love relationship between God and the women whose hearts He opened. Jesus gave us a more complete understanding of this relationship as He demonstrated His love to those women He encountered during His earthly ministry. He spoke to us, as well as to them, of the promise of God's Spirit that would come after He had ascended to His Father in heaven.

It is Peter, quoting the prophet Joel, who helps us understand what God has for women in these last days:

> And it shall come to pass in the last days, saith God, I will pour out of my Spirit upon all flesh: and your sons and your daughters shall prophesy, and your young men shall see visions, and your old men shall dream dreams:

> And on my servants and on my handmaidens I will pour out in those days of my Spirit: and they shall prophesy.
>
> **Acts 2:17,18**

In the following sections you will read about modern-day women whose hearts have been opened. It is important to realize that there are millions more whose stories will never be told; however, they are written in God's book of remembrance. (Mal. 3:16.)

Women Who Pray

Women pray today, as did the women on the riverbank. We too seek God's Spirit working through us so we can know His plans and His vision and His will for our lives. We seek Him in prayer for our own spiritual and material needs. We can also gather together, as Lydia and her friends did, and ask God for a greater understanding and fullness in the Church today.

Evelyn Christenson is a modern-day woman who has written about prayer in her book, *What Happens When Women Pray*.[2] She explains the impact that women can have as they enter into prayer for their lives, their families, the nation and the world.

Prayer separates the godly women from the ungodly. The ungodly look to themselves or to other philosophies for wisdom and strength. Godly women recognize that it is only God Who can provide true wisdom and strength.

Prayer is a recognition that God is God. When I awaken in the morning and pray, I am saying, "I need and want to be in communion with the One Who created me." I go to Him recognizing that because I belong to Him He knows my needs and the solution to those needs for that day.

After thanking Him for what He has done and praising Him for Who He is, I can begin bringing to Him my needs and the needs of others. As He speaks to me through my spirit and through verses of the Bible, I can go from that place of prayer in confidence, for I have committed my cares to Him and He has instructed me in how to do my part.

Women Who Listen

How mightily does God use those who are willing to listen to Him. A modern-day Lydia was Lydia Prince, a Danish schoolteacher and an agnostic who came into a life-changing experience with the Living Lord. Once Jesus entered her life, it changed dramatically as she followed His plans for her life. In 1928

---

[2]Evelyn Christenson, *What Happens When Women Pray* (USA: Victor Books, Scripture Press Publ. Inc., 1975).

she left a promising career, family, homeland and all that was familiar to her to go to what was then Palestine. She lived there during those years of unrest between Jew and Arab, prior to 1948 when Israel became a Jewish state.

Lydia was a single woman during most of her years in Palestine. Her days were spent caring for many orphans in the city of Jerusalem. She fed and cared for over 60 infants and children whom no one else wanted. Her income was meager and the environment was one of unrest: strikes, food shortages, street fighting and racial violence. She listened intently to God, Who instructed her in how to clothe, feed and protect the children in her care. She also reached out to a number of women in Palestine — loving and caring for them as well. The prayer for peace for the city of Jerusalem was always on her lips. (Ps. 122:6.) Her story is told in her autobiography, *Appointment in Jerusalem.*[3]

Listening to God in the "busyness" of this age requires more than anything else a reverence and respect for the Person and what He has to say. We must get to the point where we believe that He really has the perfect word for us in every situation. My own father has a nice, mellow speaking voice. I like to hear his voice, not only because it sounds nice but because he is my father. In the same way, we need to desire to hear God's voice and truly want to hear what He has to say to us through His Word and Spirit. It may not be what we have planned, but we can trust that it is the right way for us.

---

[3]Lydia Prince, *Appointment in Jerusalem* (Waco: A Chosen Book, Word Books, 1975).

Women of Industry

Mary C. Crowley, founder of Home Interiors and Gifts, is a woman who has a gift like Lydia's.

A number of years ago in Texas, Mary began a small home party business and developed it into a nationwide, multi-million-dollar conglomerate. Her faith and trust in God guided her as she pursued her business career. She did not try to separate her faith from her business. Her goal was to help American women put God first in their homes, family lives and careers. She believed that by making a home a clean and attractive place to live, the family could develop its God-given potential. She taught many of the Proverbs 31 principles as she showed women how to decorate their homes with the many items she offered for sale.

Mary shared her earnings with her employees. She offered substantial bonuses to those who gave their best effort. She never tired of testifying, to customers and employees alike, of God's providence in her life.

Neither did Mary neglect to give to Christian organizations. She has given generously to many such ministries over the years. She was the first woman to sit on the board of directors of the Billy Graham Evangelistic Association.

In her book, *You Can Too*,[4] Mary tells how she achieved success and fulfilled her dreams. Even though she endured an unhappy childhood, she

---

[4]Mary C. Crowley, *You Can Too* (Old Tappan: Power Books, Fleming H. Revell Company, 1976, 1980).

demonstrates how the love of Jesus can produce a loving and fulfilled heart.

Women of Action

Lydia took action by being baptized, encouraging her own household to believe and offering hospitality to the apostles and other Christians. There are many ways to take action, depending on the woman and her circumstances.

Freda Lindsay is one of these women of action today. She spent years working beside her husband Gordon in his ministry of evangelist, pastor, writer and founder of Christ For the Nations (CFN), a full-Gospel missionary society which has helped build nearly 4,000 churches.

After her husband's death in 1973, Freda (through godly counsel) became the president of CFN, as well as the head of Christ for the Nations Institute (CFNI) in Dallas, Texas. Over the years this school has sent out thousands of young persons equipped to carry out the ministry of Jesus Christ in the nations of the world.

Freda was not sure if she could do the challenging work that was set before her, and yet God instructed her and encouraged her day by day. This is how God works in our lives, as we are willing to accept His challenges. He equips us with what we need for the time. God does not start us off as Bible school presidents any more than He started Freda that way. He starts us off doing those things that are needed for that time and season in our life.

Freda's autobiography, *My Diary Secrets*[5] is an inspiring book for those who desire to be women of action.

Women of Courage in Time of Trial

Trials come in all sizes and shapes and are of all intensities and duration. We find that it is the trying of our faith that brings about maturity. (1 Pet. 5:10; James 1:3,12.)

When I have been tempted to despair over trials, I am reminded of a woman who was perfected in the most difficult of trials. Corrie ten Boom is a name most of us know well. You may have read her books, including *The Hiding Place*,[6] which so vividly chronicles the Christian witness of this woman who was sent to a Nazi concentration camp because she sheltered Jews during World War II.

We can learn from Corrie how to endure trials and come out better than when we went into them. If anyone had reason to be bitter, it was Corrie; and yet, through God's grace, she was able to overcome a horrible experience with a forgiving spirit toward her captors.

Not only did she benefit personally from her dependence on God during those years in a concentration camp, but she was able to help numerous other women prisoners. In the years after her release, she helped set captives free — people who, although themselves never having been in a concentration

---

[5]Mrs. Gordon Lindsay, *My Diary Secrets* (Dallas: Christ For the Nations, Inc., 1976).

[6]Corrie ten Boom, *The Hiding Place* (Lincoln: Chosen Books, 1971).

camp, were prisoners of their unforgiveness toward those who had mistreated them.

10
Gifts Differing According to Grace

Priscilla (Acts 18:1-28; Rom. 16:3; 1 Cor. 16:19; 2 Tim. 4:19.)

New Testament women are varied in looks, personalities, gifts and callings; yet there is one abiding principle in their lives, and that is the fact that Jesus set them free. (John 8:32; 2 Cor. 3:17.)

These women are illustrated in the pages of the New Testament, in Church history and in present-day lives — all those who believe in and adhere to Christ are New Testament women.

Priscilla was one of these women set free in Christ. She and her husband Aquila shared the Good News in many of the cities of the ancient province of Asia. Other women must have been encouraged by her life. Surely the entire Church knew that she was a bold witness, for both she and her husband risked their lives to help Paul with his mission to the Gentiles.

Priscilla

Priscilla as a Tentmaker

The first time we meet the woman, Priscilla, is in the home and shop where she and her husband Aquila worked at their tentmaking craft:

> **After this [Paul] departed from Athens and went to Corinth.**
>
> **There he met a Jew named Aquila, a native of Pontus, recently arrived from Italy with Priscilla his wife, due to the fact that Claudius had issued an edict that all the Jews were to leave Rome. And [Paul] went to see them;**
>
> **And because he was of the same occupation he stayed with them, and they worked [together], for they were tentmakers by trade.**
>
> **Acts 18:1-3 AMP**

It is often assumed that Priscilla and Aquila were already of the Christian faith when Paul met them; however, we do not know when or how they first embraced the Gospel. It is unlikely that Paul would have sought a working relationship with non-believers. It would have been like him to choose Priscilla and Aquila for their ardent dedication to the Christian way, as well as for their skill as tentmakers. Paul knew his course and what lay ahead. He joined with those who would help him spread the Gospel in the Gentile world in the most effective way possible.

It is interesting to note that Paul and his new friends spent the work week engaged in the craft of tentmaking. It was on the Sabbath that Paul went to the Jewish synagogue to attempt to win both Jews and Greeks to the Christian faith. (Acts 18:4.) It is not difficult to picture the three of them — Paul, Priscilla and Aquila — making tents in the midst of the busy city with its commercial and manufacturing enterprises.

Located on the Isthmus of Corinth, the city formed the most direct communication between the

Ionian and Aegean Seas. Its wealth was known, as were its many vices. The worship of Venus was accompanied by moral corruption. Priscilla and Aquila established their work in Corinth after having been driven out of Rome.

Priscilla and Aquila must have learned a great deal about cooperation from their tentmaking craft, which later helped them to cooperate in furthering the spread of the Gospel.

I have watched a husband and wife team work with canvas. Even the initial measuring takes two people working side by side. When the time comes for handling the large expanses of canvas, each must do his part in order for the pieces to be evenly joined together. It takes a "developed eye" to know when the other person needs an extra piece of canvas drawn toward him, and when a slight pull of the hand will curve out the cloth to make a well-rounded corner. This husband and wife must have developed a good communication system during those years that they were learning and practicing their craft.

In his youth, Paul, as all young Jewish boys of his time, had learned a craft as well as the Old Testament law. His forefathers, like Aquila's, had dwelt in tents until their return from Egypt to Canaan when some had begun living in cities. Now, centuries later, Paul and Aquila could earn their living with this useful skill. Priscilla had obviously been taught it as well, for she worked alongside the men.

Corinth was a strategic spot for travelers, and those who came to the home and shop of Priscilla and Aquila were from all parts of the Mediterranean region. Perhaps the couple worked cloth for ships as well. It was a necessary material for sails; one that was constantly in need of being repaired or replaced, as the water and winds wore away upon it.

What a mixed group of people must have come to this shop in Corinth. Certainly they must have walked away not only with their completed products in hand, but with a picture of an unusual threesome — Paul, Priscilla and Aquila — full of life and working in harmony. They also carried away a new teaching: one that proclaimed that the Lord God cared so much for them that He had sent His Son to die for their sins so they could be a free and forgiven people.

We can picture the one path from their tent-makers shop traveled by those who took this message to heart — herders, merchants; men and women — walking down that new path of peace and eternal life. The other dark pathway was traveled by those who did not let the message reach their hearts. They traveled back down the hopeless path to look to the goddess Venus who could offer them nothing.

How exciting and action-filled the days must have been for Priscilla as she worked with her husband and Paul during the 18 months that he stayed in Corinth. Each week Paul went to the synagogue, and surely Priscilla and Aquila went with him to hear him present his arguments to the Jews that Jesus is the Christ. How heart-wrenching it must have been to hear Paul finally tell the Jews that, because they had abused and reviled him and not taken to heart what he said, he would turn to preach to the Gentiles in Corinth. (Acts 18:6.)

Now Priscilla and Aquila found themselves not only alienated by empires like Rome because they were Jews, but also alienated from their fellow Hebrews in Corinth because they believed that Jesus was the promised Messiah. They could take comfort in a few converts from among the Jews, and the many Corinthians who believed and were baptized.

Priscilla's heart must have leaped when she heard Paul repeat the word of wisdom that he had received in a vision:

> **And one night the Lord said to Paul in a vision, Have no fear, but speak and do not keep silent;**
>
> **For I am with you, and no man shall assault you to harm you; for I have many people in this city.**
>
> Acts 18:9,10 AMP

Paul did go ahead with his work, and during the time he spent in their home and shop, Paul trained this couple to be what he later described as his "helpers in Christ." (Rom. 16:3.) How quickly the days of tentmaking must have gone as he taught them the doctrines of this New Covenant. The knowledge of Christ was growing in them, and they began imitating the life Paul lived and taught. He encouraged them both, for he saw in Priscilla and Aquila the willingness to risk it all — everything they were and everything they had — for the Gospel of Christ.

After a period of time, the Jews stirred up trouble for Paul and actually brought him before the judge's seat. In the midst of this tremendous work was great difficulty and strife. Paul must have warned Priscilla and Aquila to be ready to suffer for the Gospel, as he warned all believers. They had been instructed to be hardened against man's accusations. He taught them how to be content regardless of the state of things.

Priscilla now had the opportunity to put into practice those things she had been taught. She couldn't let anxieties unnerve her. Instead, she looked to God for His peace in the midst of this persecution that came to their household.

Priscilla as a Teacher

After Paul had established the work in Corinth, he set sail for Syria accompanied by Priscilla and Aquila. It was time for Paul to visit churches in other cities, and he now had with him his trusted helpers. He continued to enter the synagogues to proclaim the news that the Messiah had come. He also met with the churches to impart to them new strength and encouragement.

Paul left Priscilla and Aquila behind in Ephesus, as he continued on his missionary journey. They had their work cut out for them, for Ephesus was the center of the worship of the goddess Diana. Rising above the other buildings in the city was the temple of Diana, built with pledges from devotees from all over the province of Asia.

Even though Priscilla had dwelt among idolaters in every city, the sight of the temple of Diana from the harbor entrance must have given her an indication of the strength of the opposition she and Aquila would have to face there. As she gazed from the side of the ship toward the great city, perhaps she looked forward to the challenge of demonstrating that even the pagan gods were subject to the name of Jesus. Now, above all times, she needed to put on the armor that Paul described in his letter to that city.

As she worked and taught in the city of Ephesus, so full of magic arts and pagan worship, no doubt this verse was made real to Priscilla: **For we wrestle not against flesh and blood, but against principalities, against powers, against the rulers of the darkness of this world, against spiritual wickedness in high places** (Eph. 6:12).

Priscilla and Aquila remained in Ephesus while Paul visited many of the churches between that city and the route to Jerusalem. It was during this time that an issue of concern began surfacing among some of the believers. The Gospel writers continually mention the propensity of many of the people in the early churches to turn back to the Jewish law. Some who considered themselves teachers introduced into the assemblies Old Testament teachings (such as the necessity of circumcision) which no longer applied to New Testament believers. Others brought in old wives' tales and genealogies, thereby detracting from the truth of the Gospel which proclaims that Jesus is the way, the truth and the life. (John 14:6.)

While in Ephesus, Priscilla and Aquila heard a young man speak with knowledge and enthusiasm about the Gospel, but they quickly recognized that he did not have a complete knowledge of the Christian faith. He was teaching about the Lord accurately, but he did not yet have all the teaching that was necessary. They knew that someone as favored as this man could easily sway some in the Church to an inaccurate understanding of Christian baptism. We read of this incident in Acts 18:24-26 (AMP):

> **Meanwhile there was a Jew named Apollos, a native of Alexandria, who came to Ephesus. He was a cultured and eloquent man, well versed and mighty in the Scriptures.**
>
> **He had been instructed in the way of the Lord, and burning with spiritual zeal, he spoke and taught diligently and accurately the things concerning Jesus, though he was acquainted only with the baptism of John.**
>
> **He began to speak freely — fearlessly and boldly — in the synagogue; but when Priscilla and Aquila heard him, they took him with them and expounded to him the way of God more definitely and accurately.**

Priscilla was not afraid to correct this learned man, but was zealous to expound the truth. She had shown herself approved, and now she was able to help another understand more clearly.

In this one incident, we can see that Priscilla's motivation was to teach, for teaching is evidence of a desire to clarify truth. Priscilla and Aquila were sensitive to teaching that was incomplete and therefore inaccurate. They were willing to instruct Apollos in the systematic way of a gifted teacher. Apollos received their teaching, for he went from them with letters of approval and proved to be a powerful witness for the Lord. It is no wonder that Paul let all the churches know of his sincere love for this couple.

Priscilla as a Giver

Many authors comment on the fact that, in three instances (Acts 18:18; Rom. 16:3; 2 Tim. 4:19),

Priscilla's name is mentioned before that of her husband Aquila. Two of these instances are attributed to Paul. These did not go unnoted, even by the early Church. The significance of the order of the names is the fact that in Paul's time the husband was always addressed first.

To understand Paul's reversal of this established order, we need to be reminded of the scripture in which he points out that in Christ there is neither male nor female. (Gal. 3:28.) It was not as a wife that Priscilla was receiving "first billing," and therefore greater importance, but as a Christian worker. On these occasions, Paul recognized her contribution to be the greater of the two. The significant thing is that Priscilla and Aquila were a team. They each had different gifts, as do many couples today.

It may have concerned others whose name was listed first, but it was probably of no concern to Priscilla and Aquila. Their freedom in Christ allowed them to function as a team, each contributing what had been given to them by God alone in the first place. It was He Who had called and equipped them both. If Priscilla was the more gifted of the two in the ministry, it did not affect their relationship. Their main concern was for Christ's plan for their lives, and not their own. Freely they had received, and now freely they were willing to give.

The verses containing Paul's greetings to Priscilla and Aquila, and the two longer passages already discussed, are the only scriptural references we have to help us gain insight into their work in the Church. These passages provide quite a bit of information, for in titling Priscilla and Aquila as "fellow workers," Paul provides us with strong evidence that their ministry complemented his. We know that they experienced many of the same joys and sufferings that Paul describes so well in his epistles.

One of Paul greetings helps us understand another contribution which Priscilla and Aquila made to the Church:

> **The churches of Asia salute you. Aquila and Priscilla salute you much in the Lord, with the church that is in their house.**
>
> **1 Corinthians 16:19**

One of the main themes we see reoccurring throughout Priscilla's life is the opening of her home to guests. Not only did she take in Paul, but she also received others as guests. Whenever Priscilla and Aquila became established in a community, they opened their home to the members of the Church. What a blessed place their house must have been. We can envision the warmth and peace of their home, as described in Paul's words to the Colossians:

> **Let the peace of Christ rule in your hearts, since as members of one body you were called to peace. And be thankful. Let the word of Christ dwell in you richly as you teach and admonish one another with all wisdom, and as you sing psalms, hymns and spiritual songs with gratitude in your hearts to God.**
>
> **Colossians 3:15,16 NIV**

Love must have flowed freely from this woman, as she worked alongside her husband and the other disciples. Other women must have looked to her with great respect and love. Here was a woman who was not only strong in the Word, but strong in love. She taught in love, and she opened her home in love.

Obviously Paul himself had great admiration for her, for twice in his greetings he calls her Prisca, a name of endearment reserved for special friends.

Priscilla as a Risktaker

Paul wrote his letter to the Romans, and then entrusted it to a woman named Phoebe, who was a servant or a deaconness (depending on the translation) in the church at Cenchrae. Whatever her title, it is plain from Paul's remarks that her function was one of key importance to the church. Phoebe was a remarkable woman, one who had earned Paul's confidence, as well as the confidence of the many believers she had helped. Included in Paul's introduction of her is a greeting to Priscilla and Aquila, who were now back in Rome:

> **Give my greetings to Prisca and Aquila, my fellow workers in Christ Jesus,**
>
> **Who risked their lives — endangering their very necks — for my life. To them not only I but also all the churches among the Gentiles give thanks.**
>
> **Romans 16:3,4 AMP**

We know from the scriptures above that Priscilla and Aquila were willing to risk their very lives for Paul. What kind of woman risks her neck for another? Certainly one who is Christlike.

Just what kind of risks did Priscilla take? Was she exposed to some of the same treatment that Paul endured for the sake of the Gospel? Was she insulted, imprisoned, smitten, robbed, beaten, shipwrecked, stoned, in danger from water, from people, in the city and in the wilderness? Did she suffer hunger, weariness, sleeplessness, cold and lack of clothing as did

Paul? (2 Cor. 11:22-27.) She probably did not suffer all of these things, as Paul makes it clear that he suffered more than anyone. It is conceivable that she was willing to suffer all of these. It is doubtful that she put any qualifications on how far she would go in protecting Paul's life with her own.

In order for Priscilla to come to the position of risking her life for the Gospel, she had to take some other smaller risks along the way. When she made the decision to follow The Way, she risked all things: home, money, reputation, family, friends, career, comfort and ambitions. She had to be willing to give up any or all of these things. Each step along the way, she was tested and found to be true. This is remarkable, for as we read the letters of Paul, we find that many others deserted him when the going got rough. They were not ready to risk it all. They were not willing to pay the price of suffering and sacrifice.

Priscilla is a model in tentmaking, teaching, giving and risktaking for all women in the Body of Christ today.

Gifts Differing Today

Tentmaking Today

It is in those day-to-day exchanges with others that our lives are shaped and molded. Our tentmaking experiences prepare us for all other ministry, for indeed it is our daily ministry. It is in the home, the community and the workplace that we put our God-given instruction into practice. Here is the setting in which we demonstrate true discipleship.

Priscilla and Aquila worked at their tentmaking trade together. Priscilla learned what it meant to submit to Aquila as her husband. They also learned to submit to one another. (Eph. 5:21.) Their earnings depended on how well they could work together. More importantly, the success of their marriage depended on this harmonious working relationship. Their early attempts at working their trade together were probably not friction-free. Certainly they must have run into some of the same disagreements and misunderstandings that husbands and wives encounter as they work side by side today.

How much easier it must have been to work in agreement together after they began living for Christ. They had His Spirit to teach them a better, more loving way. Now they could understand that there was an important reason to eliminate strife and to live in peace. It was even more important than making and selling tents.

Many couples today work as a team. Farmers, professionals, business people, pastors and craftspeople are but a few of the husband and wife teams. It is important for married couples to learn to work together, whether or not they share the same line of work. Recreational activities or volunteer work can bring a husband and wife together in a team effort which will teach them new skills of cooperation.

For an increasing number of women, tentmaking is both in the workplace and at home. Even as Priscilla worked at a craft, she too had a home to keep. It is evident in several passages that theirs was a home of hospitality, one in which not only the family members were fed and nourished but where others could come and receive natural and spiritual food. The dual role was a demanding one then, and it is a demanding one today. It is one that should be attempted and carried out only with guidance from and total dependence upon the Lord. He is the One Who can help us set our priorities and strengthen us for the tasks at hand.

Priscilla touched the lives of many in the busy city of Corinth. There were other craftspeople, customers, visitors and all the passersby who observed this woman devoted to the Christian Way. How did she handle the scoffer? the harlot? the difficult customer? Certainly not like the other craftspeople in the district. Surely her speech and manner were different. She had given up the attitudes and manners of the old life and had clothed herself in Christ.

In order to turn our tentmaking experiences into rewarding labor, we should follow Paul's advice in Colossians, Chapter 3: We must get our minds off the difficult employer or spouse by putting our thoughts on things above. Rid ourselves of all those things like anger, bad feelings and rage as they surface at home or on the job, for most certainly they will surface. Start our day at home and at work by clothing ourselves with the "new" spirit. Remind ourselves in the supermarket, meeting place and family room that we are *His* representatives. Be gentle and patient with that whimpering child, competitive co-worker or angry driver. Forgive others and go on from there, because we have been forgiven. Allow love and peace to rule our daily lives. Take that "word" that the Lord has given us in our early morning devotions and let it train us. Sing in our hearts hymns, psalms and spiritual songs while the world sings a different tune. Live above the circumstances in any setting, as we do our work in the name of the Lord Jesus and in complete reliance upon Him.

Teaching Today

> **Having then gifts differing according to the grace that is given to us, whether prophecy, let us prophesy according to the proportion of faith;**
>
> **Or ministry, let us wait on our ministering: or he that teacheth, on teaching;**
>
> **Or he that exhorteth, on exhortation: he that giveth, let him do it with simplicity; he that ruleth, with diligence; he that sheweth mercy, with cheerfulness.**
>
> **Romans 12:6-8**

Certain women have been endowed with the gift of teaching. It seems likely that Priscilla was one of these women. During my years as a trainer of teachers in a public university, I have taught others how to teach. However, I recognize that God "gifts" those who teach His Word. Perhaps you are one of those who have been "gifted" to teach.

Aside from those who have been especially gifted as teachers of the Word of God, there rests on each of us the need to share the Good News with others. In that sense we are all teachers. Paul tells Timothy to bid the older women to teach the younger women good things. (Titus 2:3-5.) Mothers and fathers are told to teach their children. We are to encourage and exhort other members of the Body of Christ. These efforts all require teaching on our part.

The only way we can successfully teach others is by being schooled in those areas ourselves. We become schooled in the things of God by studying His Word and putting it into practice in our daily lives.

Giving Today

As with the teacher, there is in the Body of Christ the giver. Although there are people who "live to give," all members of the Body of Christ need to learn to give. As women, God has endowed us with giving hearts toward our families. As Christians, it is important that we develop giving hearts toward others as well. In the Bible we are particularly urged to give to others in the Christian faith and to the poor.

It takes wisdom to know what direction our giving should take. Prayerful decision must be made about our giving, for we can give to one person that which should have gone to another.

One of the obvious ways we can give is through our finances, but there are some things we can give without great monetary cost to us. The most important gifts we can make to others are our love and our prayers. The gifts listed in the Romans passage of the section on teaching (above) are bestowed upon us for us to share with the rest of the Body of Christ.

Risktaking Today

Risktaking is not a word that is often associated in some people's minds with women, and yet as Christian women we must be able to risk what we have in order to gain what God has for us.

Priscilla was a woman who was willing to risk her life for the Apostle Paul. As we look at other women in the Bible, we see them as risktakers as well.

Hannah risked her only son by pledging him to God, not knowing if she would ever have other children. Ruth risked her peace and security by moving to a land where she might not be accepted because of her national origin. She also risked her reputation when she went to the threshing floor to lie down under Boaz' robe. Sarah risked lifetime captivity by allowing herself to be taken into the kings' harems. She also risked her life by her willingness to become pregnant and give birth to a son at age 90. Mary of Bethany risked being misunderstood by those around her, as she poured out the perfumed ointment on the feet of Jesus. Other unnamed women of faith risked their lives. (Read Hebrews 11:35-40 for a serious account of what all our forefathers and foremothers risked for the sake of their faith.)

As we seek to know the Lord better each day, He gives us the opportunity to let go of what we hold in our hands so that He might fill them with what He has in His hand. It is our realization of His goodness that allows us to risk what we are and what we have by exchanging it for what He has for us. We can know that His exchange program is better than all others.

Many years ago, God spoke through the prophet Isaiah to give us an example of His exchange program. This is what He offers us: liberty in place of our captivity, comfort in exchange for our bereavement, beauty for ashes, the oil of joy for mourning, and the garment of praise for the spirit of heaviness. (Is. 61:1-3.) What do we have to lose when we take part in such a marvelous exchange program?

11
Living in Sincere Faith

Lois and Eunice (Acts 16:1-3; 2 Timothy 1:5; 3:14,15.)

In his second letter to Timothy, Paul wrote: **I have been reminded of your sincere faith, which first lived in your grandmother Lois and in your mother Eunice and, I am persuaded, now lives in you also** (2 Tim. 1:5 NIV).

Timothy was Lois and Eunice's letter of recommendation to the world, for these women could say to Timothy as Paul did to the Corinthian church, **You...are our letter, written on our hearts, known and read by everybody** (2 Cor. 3:2 NIV). It is a sobering thought that people will read our children (and their children) as letters and by them will commend us as mothers and grandmothers.

Faith Lives First in Lois and Eunice

Without sincere faith, it would have been a difficult life for these women. Eunice, Timothy's mother, was a Jewess and a believer who was living in Lystra when Paul first met her and her family. Timothy's father was a Greek, but that is all we know of him. (Acts 16:1.) Since Paul refers only to the mother and grandmother, it is probable that Timothy's early training came from them. Although the mixed marriage of Jew and Gentile was not uncommon at the time, it still was not well accepted by Orthodox Jews.

The responsibility of training the young boy in God's commandments fell upon the women. If Timothy's father was not living, the women also had the responsibility of providing a living for themselves and the child. It could not have been an easy life, any more than single-parenting is today. The reason that these women could face the difficult task of raising Timothy alone was that they were grounded in their faith in God.

Edith Deen, commenting on mothers of the Bible, notes that in the summary of the reign of each king of Judah and Israel, the name of the mother of each man is followed by an evaluation of her son's reign. Of some it is said, "And he did that which was right in the sight of the Lord," and of others it is said, "And he did that which was evil in the sight of the Lord."[1]

The importance of a mother's influence for good or evil did not escape Lois and Eunice. They knew full well that a mother and grandmother had great influence on the type of man a small boy would become.

One of the most significant points in Paul's commendation of Lois and Eunice was his observation that sincere faith dwelled *first* in them. Before Lois and Eunice could help Timothy develop into the man he would become, they had to have faith in God. A mother's faith must be firmly established before she can help to establish it in her child. To raise a young man who was recommended by the elders of

---

[1]Edith Deen, *All the Women of the Bible* (New York: Harper & Brothers, 1955) pp. 221-222.

the city was quite an accomplishment. (Acts 16:2.) For Paul himself to desire Timothy to travel with him on his missionary journeys must have been elating for the women. All the years of loving and training Timothy had paid off. He now had a father in Paul who could complete the work that his faithful mother and grandmother had begun so well.

Timothy Trained in the Word

As we read the letters to Timothy, we find Paul advising this young man on sound doctrine for the churches he had entrusted to him. He warns him not to let people despise his youthfulness, but to live such a godly life that they will respect him. Over and over within the recommendation that Paul is writing to his young charge, we hear an overtone of love. Timothy's nature had been molded by his grandmother and mother into one that inspired a great fatherly love for the apostle.

We can imagine that the household in which Timothy grew up was one full of warmth and care. As soon as he was old enough to hear Bible stories about Noah and David and Ruth, no doubt Lois pulled him onto her knee and told them to him. Like all young children, Timothy was surely more interested in certain stories than others. He, like all toddlers, would probably sit a while and then move on to something else.

It seems evident that the women did not depend on these little teaching sessions alone, but told Timothy of the goodness of God as seen in all the everyday occurrences of life. When Eunice would come home from the market with a good buy for the day, she would doubtless thank *Jehovah-Jireh*, Who provided for them. When they would hear a bad report from another part of the city, they would certainly have given thanks to *Jehovah-Nissi*, Who was their banner and protection over them. When they nursed young Timothy through childhood illnesses, they would have called upon the name of *Jehovah-Rapha*, the God Who heals. Paul indicates in his letters that Timothy knew his heavenly Father from the time he was little more than a baby.

As he grew, Timothy must have enjoyed bringing other boys home with him. What interest the young pagan children must have taken in this household. Here the women smiled, sang and talked to their God as they worked. They did not curse nor route young boys out of the house with a stick. They had a smile on their face and a love in their eye that was not within the young boys' experience to understand. Timothy must have been the one to explain their strange behavior to the boys. He could tell them about the love of God, and then point to it on the face of his mother and grandmother.

As Timothy continued to grow toward young manhood, Lois and Eunice began teaching him from the scriptures. They must have known that these words would keep him when the two of them were no longer able to watch over him. It is likely that they were convinced that Timothy would be able to lead a godly life, even within this Gentile country, if he kept the commandments. In fact, Paul reinforced this belief many years later when he was being persecuted for his faith and witness. He told Timothy that evil men would go from bad to worse, exhorting him:

> **But as for you, continue in what you have learned and have become convinced of, because you know those from whom you learned it, and how from infancy you have known the holy Scriptures, which are able to make you wise for salvation through faith in Christ Jesus. All Scripture is God-breathed and is useful for teaching, rebuking, correcting and training in righteousness, so that the man of God may be thoroughly equipped for every good work.**
>
> **2 Timothy 3:14-17 NIV**

Paul knew that Eunice and Lois had begun teaching Timothy scriptures when he was still an infant. He probably also knew that within this loving household there was discipline — not always perfect discipline, but the women knew that God's commandments were useful for correction and discipline. (Prov. 6:23.)

Clearly, Eunice and Lois were familiar with the Bible accounts of indulgent parents and the resulting heartaches their children brought to their lives. They knew of Eli the priest who did not correct his sons' evil ways, and as a result lost all of them to death, leaving none from his family to continue in the priesthood. (1 Sam. 3:13.) They saw how David did not correct his son Adonijah at any time, and the young man rebelled against his father and tried to make himself king. (1 Kings 1:5,6.)

Paul's letters to Timothy outline some basic truths that he obviously felt had to be brought to the young man's remembrance. Paul, along with the women, was one who taught Timothy. We do not know at what time in Timothy's life he received Christ as Savior, but we know that the truths of the New

Testament were completing the work begun early in his life.

In his writing, Paul instructed Timothy lovingly, following the same advice that he had written to fathers in the churches at Ephesus and Collosae:

> **And, ye fathers, provoke not your children to wrath; but bring them up in the nurture and admonition of the Lord.**
>
> **Ephesians 6:4**

> **Fathers, provoke not your children to anger, lest they be discouraged.**
>
> **Colossians 3:21**

Timothy received the Word of God from Paul, Lois and Eunice with discipline and love.

Motherhood Requires Change

After hearing good reports of Timothy from the elders in Lystra and Derbe, Paul decided to take him along on his missionary journeys. From that day forward, life was forever changed for Eunice and Lois. Their Timothy was a man now and no longer in their charge.

This did not happen all at once, although it probably seemed that way when Paul began talking to the women about Timothy's part in his travel plans. It had been a while in coming, this moment of separation and departure. God had been preparing their hearts for this day all along the way. Timothy had already gained the respect of the brothers by his pleasant demeanor and his knowledge of the scriptures. (Acts 16:2.) No doubt, Lois and Eunice had seen less and less of him as the Church began growing. Certainly, it was what they had prayed for, "God use this boy for Your glory." Now they must have known that the Lord had heard them and had prepared a very special place for him.

When the time came for Timothy to leave, it was doubtless a day mixed with joy and sadness. Like other women in ages past, Lois and Eunice had poured so much of themselves in time and energy and love into this young man, and now it was time to back away and let him go. As John the Baptist told the crowds, "I must decrease and he (Christ) must increase." (John 3:30.)

Lois and Eunice obviously knew that if they had truly done their job correctly during the early years of Timothy's life, now was the appropriate time to release him into the calling God had chosen for him. This did not mean that their importance to his life was diminished, but that their direct involvement in his life had to decrease. They had likely prayed for a father figure for Timothy to help him in his young adult years, and now it seems that God had responded by giving them the best. They had a joy in their hearts. Why should they be teary-eyed?

The joy and sadness of the women were surely mingled in those first few days after Timothy had left with Paul and Silas. The realization of their new role in his life would not have hit them all at once. It was over the period of the next few years that they could likely begin seeing the good seed they had planted in his young life take root and grow.

Prayer had always been a part of their life. They had prayed earnestly and consistently during those early years. Their intercession was needed now more than ever. This is how they would assist Timothy in the many years he remained as a worker with Paul — they would pray and intercede for him.

A compact biography of Timothy's life shows us that he was faithful to Paul until the end. He started learning from Paul the day he joined the apostle on his second missionary journey. One Bible scholar tells us of Timothy:

"He shared in the evangelization of Macedonia and Achia and aided Paul during the three years of preaching at Ephesus, where he became thoroughly acquainted with the city and with the needs of the local church. He was one of the delegates appointed to Jerusalem (Acts 20:4) and probably went with Paul all the way back to that city. He was with Paul in Rome during the first imprisonment, for his name appears in the headings of Colossians (1:1) and of Philemon (1). After the release, he traveled with Paul and evidently was left at Ephesus to straighten out the tangle that had developed there, while Paul went on to visit the churches in Macedonia. At the end of Paul's life he joined him at Rome (2 Tim. 4:11,21) and himself suffered imprisonment (Heb. 13:23), from which he was later released."[2]

As we can see from this short summary of Timothy's life, over the years Lois and Eunice had marvelous opportunities to pray. They could have taken the imprisonments, the riots and the difficult journeys as opportunities to worry (and perhaps they did for a fleeting time), but it was not in the character

---

[2]Merrill C. Tenney, *New Testament Survey* (Grand Rapids: Wm. B. Eerdmans Publishing Company, 1961) p. 334.

of these women to believe that their worry would bring them the end-result they desired. They shared in the desire to see the Gospel preached in the known world, and they must have known that this would not come to pass without sacrifice. They also had to know that their Timothy was a part of that sacrifice.

In those precious times when Timothy did join them in their home as he passed through Lystra must have been moments of unsurpassed joy. How eagerly they must have listened to all he had to say about his work in the churches. They surely made the most of those days, giving him the encouragement he needed, and preparing the special foods they had fed him as a child. When he left, they no doubt urged him to write a letter when he had time so they would know how he was faring. Each time a traveler entered their church after having seen Timothy, how hungrily they must have listened to the report of their beloved son and grandson.

Lois and Eunice Rejoice

It is left to our imagination what Lois and Eunice and the other women of the Bible looked like. Certainly joy is one quality that would have described their character. The reason we can know this is because the Lord promises joy to the parents of a wise child:

> **My son, if your heart is wise,**
> **then my heart will be glad;**
> **my inmost being will rejoice**
> **when your lips speak what is right....**
>
> **The father of a righteous man has great joy;**
> **he who has a wise son delights in**
> **him.**

**May your father and mother be glad;
may she who gave you birth rejoice!**
Proverbs 23:15,16,24,25 NIV

Lois and Eunice had some choices to make that all women must make as their sons and daughters go out on their own. They could worry and fret, or they could be confident and rejoice in Timothy's work in the Gospel. They could try to hang on to Timothy and direct his life as they had done when he was a child, or they could say, "We have done our best, and now he must learn to guide his own steps." They could rest on the laurels of having raised a good son and grandson, or they could continue in the faith.

Living in Sincere Faith Today

Faith Must First Be in Us

It is by our faith, as women, wives and mothers, that we will see God's will accomplished in our lives: **But without faith it is impossible to please him: for he that cometh to God must believe that he is, and that he is a rewarder of them that diligently seek him** (Heb. 11:6.)

What does your family need? What do you hope for? You can know that it is through faith that you will receive those things: **Now faith is the substance of things hoped for, the evidence of things not seen** (Heb. 11:1). Remember the word that the angel spoke to Sarah and to Mary? "With God all things are possible."

Whatever you hope for (a believing spouse; a godly marriage; children living for God; protection from harm; clothing, shelter and food needs met) can be received through faith. Faith is the substance of those things hoped for and the evidence of those things not yet seen. God will be pleased by your faith and will reward you with those things you hope for as you seek Him. Until you receive your reward, your faith must be the evidence in your life.

Lois and Eunice by faith taught Timothy the scriptures, loved him and supported him. It was not until he became a man that they had the full evidence that he would serve God. They continued day by day to believe God for their physical and spiritual needs. That is how we walk as mothers and grandmothers in faith. We believe that God has everything we need to raise our children; and not only does He have everything, but He is willing to give it to us as we seek Him in faith. He does not withhold a thing that we need, but is generous and loving to His daughters.

What do you need for your child this day and in the days to come? Wisdom and understanding, correct answers, sound discipline, strength, love, food, clothing and healing are all available for us as we raise our children to become sound adults. If God fulfilled His promises to a faithful Timothy, the offspring of a mixed marriage in a pagan country without the benefit of a believing father, then surely we can believe God that our children will be wise and faithful.

First, sincere faith must live in us.

Training Children in the Word

Paul wrote that evil men would become worse, but Timothy did not have to be a part of that falling away from God because he had the scriptures to make him wise. Paul gives us a clue in these verses concerning the time that scriptures can be introduced to children. He said that Timothy had known them from infancy.

The very first words spoken to a child can be scripture. You can speak words like "Jesus loves you," and "God is love," from the day of your child's birth. Psychologists are recognizing a greater capacity for learning in the infant than has even been thought possible. The same is true of spiritual understanding. The infant's receptivity of spiritual things is much greater than most of us have ever dreamed.

My Christian walk was deeper by the time my first two grandchildren were born, and I was able to help train them in a way that I did not train my own children when they were small. My husband and I prayed with our grandchildren, sang with them and taught them about Jesus right from the beginning of their lives. I must add that we could do this only because our son and his wife allowed us to share in their lives. It became evident to us that very small children are extremely receptive. At a very early age, our grandchildren composed songs of praise. They memorized Bible verses. They understood truths that we have seen adults flounder over. By the age of three, they had both received Christ as Savior.

A sensitivity to the child and how he is perceiving is important in knowing what to say to him about Jesus. It is safe to say that most children perceive more than we think they do. It is also important to know the Word of God yourself so you can present Christ in just the right way for that time and that child. If you are a mother or a grandmother, pray for the wisdom and the timing to present the Gospel of Christ to the young children in your family.

There is no set formula for leading a child to a decision for Christ, nor a set age. The following is an example of how the Word of God can work in the lives of little children. This is how I shared the Gospel with my granddaughters:

Jesus Knocks at the Door of Sarah's Heart:

It was the Christmas holidays and I was watching a leading evangelist on television. Sarah, who would be three in January, was excited about the Christmas season. We had read books about the birth of Christ, and she had listened intently. Her favorite "toy" was an ornament from the dime store. It was a cheap plastic manger scene. She had it in her hand as she came into the television room and hung on the arm of my chair. She wanted to talk to me, and I tried to answer her while listening to the program.

Suddenly I realized that the program wasn't as important as what she was saying. She held the little manger scene up in her hands and told me who all the people were. "Mary, Joseph and Baby Jesus." At the back of the little stable was a door that swung open. She closed the door and said, "Knock. Knock. Baby Jesus." From my heart arose the scripture, Revelation 3:20, in which the Lord says: **Behold, I stand at the door, and knock: if any man hear my voice, and open the door, I will come in to him, and will sup with him, and he with me.**

I said, "Jesus is knocking at the door of your heart," and I touched her tiny chest. "Knock. Knock. Are you going to let Him into your heart?"

"Yes," she said, and I perceived it be a sincere yes.

We prayed together and she asked Jesus to come into her heart. I prayed, as I always do when leading someone to Christ, that she would have an assurance of her salvation. It is by believing in our hearts and confessing with our lips that we are saved. (Rom. 10:9,10.)

Later that day, my husband said to me, "Sarah came downstairs and told me and her mother and dad that she had asked Jesus to come into her heart."

Jesus Becomes Amber's Perfect Sacrifice:

On a short trip that I was making for the university, I really felt drawn to a dilapidated little restaurant off the highway. At the door I hesitated, because the place looked so run down, but I felt the Spirit leading me to go in. Inside were mainly mothers and their young children enjoying pizza and pop together. After lunch I noticed a rack of books and found them to be Christian publications. One children's book particularly caught my eye. It was about Abraham and Sarah, and was nicely illustrated. I bought it to read to my grandchildren.

Some days later, the children came to visit and I pulled them up onto my lap. Amber had just turned three. We began reading about the journey of faithful Abraham and the exciting birth of Isaac to Sarah. I could sense Amber's interest beginning to be aroused. She began patting my arm to look at me and talk, especially when we got to the part of the story where Abraham brings Isaac up to the mountain as a sacrifice.

At that point, Amber's little spirit seemed to be pulling on mine as she strained to find out what would happen to Isaac. She was ecstatic when she found that God provided a ram in the thicket to take the place of Isaac. I believe that she understood that God provided this substitute. I told her that Jesus was our sacrifice. God had provided Him so we wouldn't have to die, but could live forever with Him.

I asked Amber if she would like to receive Jesus as her own sacrifice, and she said yes. Four-year-old Sarah and I prayed with her that day. Later she went into the yard where my husband was raking and told him that Jesus was living in her heart now.

Training in the scriptures should not end in the home until the day a child establishes his or her own home. It takes a great deal of creativity and tact to bring the Word to some adolescent childen; and although other Christians may help with this task, it is still the responsibility of the parent to train his or her children in the scriptures. God set the pattern for teaching His commandments in our homes: **Impress them on your children. Talk about them when you sit at home and when you walk along the road, when you lie down and when you get up** (Deut. 6:7 NIV).

There has never been a time in our history when the Word of God has had more meaning. As the world becomes more and more complex, godly instruction for raising children becomes all the more relevant. It was written to last forever.

Motherhood Requires Change

There are two days in the life of our children that require tremendous change to take place in our role as a mother. One is the day they enter school for the first time; the other is the day they leave home. Mothers are required to give selflessly during a child's early years, and then they are required to give up that child selflessly as he reaches adulthood.

Many books have been written in recent years about the empty-nest syndrome. As a parent who has recently experienced this phenomenon, I can say that it takes numerous adjustments in attitude over a number of years. If we have truly dedicated our children to the Lord and said, as Hannah did, "I have given him to the Lord" (and of course, she actually did this before he was born), then we can have the core of the adjustment problem conquered. We can then say, "I gave the child to the Lord and for a time I took care of him. Now he is still the Lord's, and I must now learn how to be mother to an adult." Times like these require more than mother love working in us; they require *agape* (the God-kind of) love.

Lois and Eunice felt a mixture of sadness and joy as they watched young Timothy leave their home to go to evangelize the Mediterranean area for Christ. We feel that same mixture as we see our children leave home for the first time. It is a necessary thing for each of us to let go of our adult children and let them be what God intends them to be. Certainly we can still be a positive influence, but not an interference! It is through prayer and intercession that we learn the difference.

What do you do when your children are gone? The same thing I believe Lois and Eunice did — they continued to grow in the faith, going about doing good as God has instructed us to do. Life does not have to end when your children leave home; it can be a beginning for all the positive things you have desired to do. There is much to share with a world that needs the qualities of a godly mother and grandmother.

Mothers Rejoice!

Children are meant to be a blessing. (Ps. 127:3-5; Prov. 17:6.) Jesus repeatedly made known the preciousness of young children.

As Christian parents we can expect our children to bring us cause to rejoice. (Prov. 23:15,16,24,25.) Some of the rejoicing comes in later years after we see them established in God's ways, but it is also necessary for us to start rejoicing now over the small steps they take.

Every child has redeeming qualities. If you have one whose redeeming qualities are a little hard to find, it is necessary to search for them, and when you do find them to rejoice over them. We may not raise our children just the way Timothy was raised, but we can raise wise children. The wisdom becomes theirs as we teach them from God's Word and pray for them.

Bibliography

Christenson, Evelyn. *What Happens When Women Pray*. USA: Victor Books, a division of Scripture Press Publ., Inc., 1975.

Crowley, Mary C. *You Can Too*. Old Tappan: Power Books, Fleming H. Revell, 1976, 1980.

Deen, Edith. *All the Women of the Bible*. New York: Harper & Brothers, 1955.

Hess, Margaret. *Unconventional Women*. "How to Combine Business with Godliness." Wheaton: Victor Books, a division of Scripture Press Publ., Inc., 1981.

Lindsay, Gordon. *Life of Christ Series*. "Christ Teaches the Apostles," Vol. XII. Dallas: Christ for the Nations, 1971.

Lindsay, Mrs. Gordon. *My Diary Secrets*. Dallas: Christ for the Nations, Inc., 1976.

Meyer, F.B. Rev. *Through the Bible Day by Day*. Philadelphia: American Sunday-School Union, 1916.

Price, Eugenia. *God Speaks To Women Today*. Grand Rapids: Zondervan Publishing House, 1964.

Prince, Lydia. *Appointment in Jerusalem*. Waco: A Chosen Book, Word Books, 1975.

Smith, William. *A Dictionary Of The Bible*. Nashville, Camden and New York: Thomas Nelson Publishers, 1962.

ten Boom, Corrie. *The Hiding Place*. Lincoln: Chosen Books, 1971.

Thompson, Frank Charles. *The New Chain Reference Bible*. Indianapolis: B.B. Kirkbride Bible Co. Inc., 1964.

Wold, Margaret. *Women of Faith & Spirit*. Minneapolis: Augsburg Publishing House, 1987.

Notes

Notes

Notes

Notes

Notes

Notes

Notes

Notes

Notes

Notes

Notes

Notes